FRONTMAN

OBAMA'S DARKEST SECRETS REVEALED

BY VICTOR THORN

PUBLISHED BY AMERICAN FREE PRESS

FRONTMAN:
OBAMA'S DARKEST SECRETS REVEALED

ISBN: 978-0-9823448-3-5

By VICTOR THORN

PUBLISHED MAY 2010 BY
AMERICAN FREE PRESS
645 Pennsylvania Avenue SE, #100
Washington, D.C. 20003

TOLL FREE ORDERING: 1-888-699-NEWS
WEBSITE: WWW.AMERICANFREEPRESS.NET

ABOUT THE COVER:

The cover art is from the fertile imagination of talented illustrator David Dees. Dees is probably the most prolific purveyor of self-created, politically incorrect, satirical artwork working today. He can be commissioned for book covers, posters, commercial illustrations, photography and more. See his website at DeesIllustration.com for contact information and for a huge archive of samples.

TABLE OF CONTENTS

BARACK OBAMA

INTRODUCTION:

Barack Obama and the Covert Symbolism of Destruction

By Victor Thorn

Anyone who has studied the true nature of political conspiracies realizes that none of us can truly comprehend what takes place behind the scenes in the *Wizard of Oz* realm of New World Order plotters. In this sense, one of the most effective methods of viewing these individuals is via the use of symbols. In other words, if "all the world's a stage" and they are but actors in a grand illusion, then each player becomes a symbol of what is to be represented.

In this sense, Barack Obama is an extremely dangerous symbol for our nation's future. This book, compiled from articles I wrote for AMERICAN FREE PRESS between 2008 and the latter part of 2009, is one of the most comprehensive examinations of President Obama ever compiled, and serves to illustrate the destructive path his handlers are leading us along.

Barack Obama has chosen and accepted his destiny, and along with it he's dragging our country into a transformation that will forever alter our existence. This man strode into office on the mantra of "change," and because George W. Bush & Company deliberately beat us down for eight years, the gullible and naïve embraced this change. But their hope is similar to blind faith, in that nothing substantive can ever be built on a weak, baseless foundation.

Despite his charisma and charm, this president epitomizes an empty suit—a man so lacking any principle or core of his own that he's addicted to a teleprompter-proxy to deliver nearly every word of his 'message'. Envision a 21st century *Manchurian Candidate* whose technological lifeblood extends directly to Orwellian words on a video monitor. This reliance on unseen words, crafted by unseen hands and unseen minds, is the vehicle that propels us down a highway to hell.

"Don't pay attention to that man behind the curtain." But today, our presidency is just the opposite. Obama is the weak little man in front of the curtain, while the booming voice of his Oz-like globalist controllers looms through blips on an electronic screen. They pull the levers, and he dangles by their strings. He's the puppet of hope, a marionette Pied Piper leading us to a financial and spiritual Golgotha.

Although the mainstream media rarely provides a glimpse of these monsters that lurk behind the veil, in the ensuing pages you'll encounter them in their basest, most unvarnished form (motives and all). Discover Barack Obama's allegiance to the United Nations and the cloaked symbolism used in his speeches. Likewise, meet Zbigniew Brzezinski, George Soros, the Rothschild clan, and all the Bilderberg-Trilateral Commission-Council on Foreign Relations members who comprise his Cabinet. To implement their policies, a vast socialist network was erected to facilitate the ultimate merger between Big Government and the banking industry (often using deadly tactics). As a result, Fannie & Freddie trot on stage, as does universal health care, bank bailouts, and the takeover of our auto industry. Undeniably, fanaticism has reared its ugly head.

Also in all their ignominious glory are the scandals: conman Tony Rezko, black nationalist race-baiter Rev. Jeremiah Wright, Obama's gay-crack cocaine bombshell, Weather Underground terrorist William Ayers, thuggish Zionist Rahm Emanuel, disgraced Gov. Rod Blagojevich, Chicago Mob politics, and the Henry Gates fiasco where Obama showed his true racist colors.

But there's even more that's not contained within this edition. How many people know that after Obama graduated from college in 1983, he worked for a CIA cutout firm named Business International Corporation (BIC)? Our future president was employed as a researcher in this intelligence-gathering network, whereof author Wayne Madsen wrote on February 26,

2009, "Obama's tuition debt at Columbia University was paid off by BIC." Could such information be nothing more than wild conspiratorial speculation? No, because as William Blum divulges in *The Question That May Never Go Away: Who Really is Barack Obama*, the *New York Times* "disclosed in 1977 that Business International had provided cover for four CIA employees in various countries between 1955 and 1960."

Blum continues, "Not only doesn't Obama mention his employer's name [in his autobiography], he fails to say when he worked there or why he left the job. There may well be no significance to these omissions, but inasmuch as Business International has a long association with the world of intelligence, covert actions, and attempts to penetrate the radical left—including Students for a Democratic Society (SDS)—it's valid to wonder if the inscrutable Mr. Obama is concealing something about his own association with this world."

In my *Hillary (and Bill)* trilogy, I proved beyond any doubt that the Clintons were recruited into the CIA to infiltrate the student antiwar movement. Did Obama follow in their footsteps by surreptitiously becoming a part of the Agency? Len Bracken's July 2009 article, *The Invisible Currency of Fascism*, corroborates Blum's assertions. "Obama's first job out of college was as a researcher and writer for Business International Corporation, a firm with deep ties to the CIA that eventually merged with the Economist Intelligence Unit, which is said to work closely with Britain's MI-6."

Along these same lines, Obama hired Mr. Greg Craig as his White House legal counsel. Who is he? Well, Craig represented one of the most notorious CIA directors of all time—Richard Helms. He not only served as an administrator for the deadly Vietnam-era Phoenix Program, he was also instrumental in launching the mind-control nightmare known as MK-ULTRA. Craig also represented John Hinkley (Ronald Reagan's wannabe assassin), the UN's ultra-crooked Kofi Annan (oil-for-food scandal) and has worked for the Clintons and Teddy Kennedy. Is this the type of change we were promised?

Then, of course, who could ignore Obama's incestuous relationship with the financial industry? Len Bracken reminds us, "The elite that owns the government hails mostly, but not entirely, from the six banks that hold nearly all U.S. bank derivative positions: the Golden Circle formed by JP-Morgan Chase, Bank of America, Citi, Goldman Sachs, Wells Fargo, and

HSBC." The USA has never been more astronomically debt-ridden in its existence, and these very institutions that paved the way to 1600 Pennsylvania Avenue for Obama now have us in their collective death grip.

Barack Obama is a dangerous symbol: a man whose mission is to completely transform American life as we've come to know it. Once you complete this book, ask yourself a simple question: what will happen to our once-great Republic after Barack Obama and his diabolical puppet-masters complete their reign of terror? You can't un-ring a bell, and the death-knell is now chiming for America.

—VICTOR THORN
May 15, 2010
Happy Valley, Pa.

Obama a Tool of Bilderberg?

Originally published: February 14, 2008

A s AMERICAN FREE PRESS editor Jim Tucker reported in his *Bilderberg Diary*, internationalists have been trying as far back as 1992 to "establish a global UN tax" which would be used to finance their globalist-oriented programs. Of course the brunt of this UN tax would fall on the shoulders of American workers, and it now appears that Democrat Barack Obama is spearheading it.

On February 14, 2008, Obama, while still in the Senate, sponsored a bill called the "Global Poverty Act" (S 2433). It was introduced to the Senate Foreign Relations Committee after already being passed in the House. What this bill would in effect do is levy a global tax on the United States where an additional 0.7% of our GNP (Gross National Product) would be earmarked to foreign aid (on top of what we already spend). If it passed, by 2021 the U.S. would have been committed to an extra $845 billion in foreign aid.

The scenario gets worse. Not only would the United States be under the UN's thumb in regard to taxation, but this bill (part of the globalists' Millennium Development Goal) would also seek to ban certain weapons, establish an international criminal court, push global warming legislation, and promote "biological diversity." Anyone familiar with the Bilderbergers immediately realizes that all of the above "buzzwords" have been part of their agenda for decades.

Assisting Barack Obama in his endeavors are two longtime CFR members: Republican Senator Richard Lugar, who has been called Obama's mentor, and Democratic Senator Joseph Biden. To illustrate how readily these men serve as pawns for the New World Order, both have been very influential in trying to pass the UN's Law of the Sea Treaty (LOST). One political commentator has stated that this bill "would effectively turn control of seven-tenths of the Earth's surface over to the United Nations," not to mention surrendering the sovereignty of our seas to them.

As the mainstream media has been reporting with gleeful relish over the past several months, Barack Obama's popularity can be attributed to one concept: he stands for change. But is this the type of change that American citizens really want—to become enslaved by a United Nation's global tax on top of the local, state and federal taxes they already pay? It's time to rip the sheen off of Barack Obama and expose him for what he really is: another political tool whose loyalties lie with those shadowy figures who sit atop the world's control pyramid.

Barack Obama's Whitewater

Originally published: March 24, 2008

Throughout the 1990s, Bill and Hillary Clinton were hounded by a corrupt real estate scandal that came to be known as Whitewater. Now, a decade later, Barack Obama has similar troubles. On March 6, 2008, Antoin "Tony" Rezko appeared in a Chicago courtroom to face charges in a $7 million federal trial. The reason these legal proceedings affect Obama is that Rezko has been described as Obama's bagman and primary campaign fundraiser in the 2008 election. In fact, Rezko funneled so much cash to Obama that after he was indicted on fraud, extortion and money laundering charges, Obama suddenly "donated $157,835 in Rezko-linked contributions to charity."

Similar to Hillary's explanations for Whitewater, Obama dismisses his connections to Rezko as nothing more than a boneheaded mistake over a little land deal. But their ties go much deeper. Associates since 1990, Rezko's fortunes grew as his notoriety as a slumlord increased. This situation wouldn't affect Obama except for one glaring detail: most of the government-subsidized properties Rezko let deteriorate to deplorably unlivable standards were located in areas where Obama turned a blind eye as either a community organizer or state senator. In addition, Obama also performed legal work for Rezko on these properties, as well as giving an internship—at Rezko's request—to the son of John Aramanda, who was a Rezko contributor and co-conspirator in his federal corruption case.

Another incident which proves they were more than mere colleagues was a 2005 real estate deal where Obama and Rezko bought adjoining lots in a Chicago suburb, closing their deals on the same day. But when Obama wanted to increase the size of his $1.65 million property, he purchased part of Rezko's parcel from his wife Rita. Fully aware that Rezko was being investigated by the U.S. Attorney's Office when this transaction took place, Obama still went forward with the deal. Such arrangements appeared to be a trend between the two, for there is also evidence of questionable campaign financing where donors would legally contribute money to Rezko, who would then in turn reimburse Obama with laundered money (*Chicago Sun-Times*, January 8, 2008). This technique is almost identical to how the Clintons moved dirty money through the ADFA (Arkansas Development Finance Authority) to raise funds for Bill's gubernatorial elections during the 1980s.

Barack Obama's Achilles heel has now surfaced, for Rezko has also been involved in wire fraud; influence peddling; bribery; kickbacks; extorting money from companies doing business with the Illinois Teacher's Retirement Board; and highly suspect deals involving Iraqi wheeler-dealer Nadhmi Auchi, an accomplice of Saddam Hussein who's been charged with bribing various political figures in Great Britain (among many other shady endeavors). The big question now is: will the American mainstream media expose Barack Obama's skeletons, or will they continue handling him with kid gloves?

Radical Black Theology Pervades Thinking of Those Closest To Barack and Michelle Obama

Originally published: April 7, 2008

In 2008, revelations regarding Barack Obama's spiritual advisor, Rev. Jeremiah Wright, were splashed across media outlets far and wide. After Wright called our country "the U.S. KKK of A," and said that blacks should sing "God Damn America" instead of "God Bless America," an entirely new barometer was used to gauge the Democratic front-runner.

On March 18, Obama delivered a speech in Philadelphia where he told voters to reexamine the subject of racism. But after taking his advice, one discovers that Rev. Wright's race-baiting and America-hating is based on a concept called black liberation theology, founded by James Cone, author of *Black Power and Black Liberation*. Cone's extremist views are centered on the following rancor:

> Black theology refuses to accept a god who is not identified totally with the goals of the black community. If God is not for us and against white people, then he is a murderer, and we had better kill him. The task of black theology is to kill gods who do not belong to the black community. Black theology will accept only the love of a god which participates in the destruction of the white enemy.

Mirroring his mentor, James Cone, Rev. Wright says of his church—the one Barack Obama has attended for twenty years—"We are African people, and remain true to our native land, the mother continent." Now is it clear

Barack Obama poses with his longtime pastor, Jeremiah Wright.

why Obama refuses to cover his heart during the Pledge of Allegiance, or wear an American flag pin on his lapel? His loyalties are *not* to the USA.

Rev. Wright, who presented a lifetime achievement award to Louis Farrakhan in 2007, labeled blacks that boycotted the 1995 Million Man March, "Oreos, house 'niggras,' Uncle Toms, and a boatload of darkies who think in white supremacist terms." In the past, Farrakhan has called whites "blue-eyed devils" and "skunks of the planet." Wright even went so far as to blame the September 11, 2001 terrorist attacks on America. "We as a white nation brought 9-11 down on ourselves because of our violent acts." However, if Wright had any moral courage, he would have disclosed that 9-11 wasn't the fault of innocent Americans, but was orchestrated by a cabal of Israel-first neo-cons within the Bush administration, as well as elements of the Mossad.

Even Obama's wife Michelle—who quipped in 2008, "For the first time in my adult lifetime I am really proud of my country"—sees the world in very stark black versus white terms. In her college thesis, she puts forth the premise that blacks trying to assimilate into white society are sell-outs. "Separationists are more closely associated with the black lower class than are integrationists." She continued this thought. "My further integration and/or assimilation into a white culture or social structure will only allow me to remain on the periphery of society." Michelle Obama's misgivings are undeniably misguided, because in 2006 she earned nearly $275,000, while her husband is the president.

Obviously, that's not living on the periphery of society.

Throughout the primaries, Barack Obama was a blank slate. But now that his association with radical, extremist black-power racists is being revealed, Americans need to ask themselves if this is the type of man they want sitting in the White House. In a hyper-sensitive atmosphere where every instance of white racism is reported (both real and imagined), Obama refused—until pressured by his advisors—to leave his overtly racist Trinity United Church of Christ, or divorce himself from Rev. Jeremiah Wright, whose sermons inspired the title of his book, *The Audacity of Hope*. On a daily basis, Obama calls for unity, change and a color-blind society; yet his hypocrisy is glaringly apparent. Is this divisive, Marxist-oriented theology of black liberation the direction we want our nation to be heading in? If Americans want truth in government, it's time to discard political correctness and start calling a spade a spade.

Members of Obama's Church Killed Execution-Style

Originally published: June 2, 2008

Is a Barack Obama bombshell lurking in the shadows, waiting to derail one of the biggest Cinderella stories in recent history? While most political prognosticators in the mainstream press would say that Barack Obama is the presumptive Democratic nominee for president, they still wonder aloud if Hillary Clinton (or some other entity) has something to reveal.

The bombshell may involve the murder of Donald Young, a 47-year-old choirmaster at former Rev. Jeremiah Wright's Trinity United Church of Christ—the same congregation that Obama has attended for the past 20 years. In addition, two other young black men that attended the same church—Larry Bland and Nate Spencer—were also murdered execution-style with bullets to the backs of their heads—all within 40 days of each other beginning in November 2007. All three were young, black and openly gay.

What links this story to Barack Obama is that, according to Larry Sinclair, Obama is a closet bisexual with whom he had sexual and drug-related encounters in November 1999. Further, Sinclair claims that Obama was friendly with at least two of these deceased parishioners, and that choir director Donald Young had contacted him shortly before being murdered from multiple gunshot wounds on December 23, 2007.

These killings are receiving a number of different reactions. Mike Parker, reporting for CBS in Chicago, wrote, "Activists fear gay African-Americans are being targeted for murder," while Marc Loveless of the Coalition for Justice and Respect queries, "Are we under attack? Is this a serial killer?"

An even more sinister aspect of this case is being investigated. According to Larry Sinclair in an affidavit to the Chicago Police Department, Donald Young had informed him that he and Barack Obama were "intimate" with each other. Sinclair, it should be noted, declared on a January 18, 2008 *YouTube* video that on two separate occasions in November 1999, he had sexual relations with Obama, and that Obama smoked crack cocaine—once in a limousine, and the other at a hotel in Gurnee, Illinois.

Larry Sinclair has also asked: why would Donald Young—whom he had never met—initiate these calls by contacting him on cell phone numbers known only in the Obama camp? Further, a private investigator connected to the Chicago Police Department told the *Globe*, "Donald Young was silenced because of something he knew about Obama. Donald was in a position where he heard a lot of things and saw a lot of things concerning Barack."

Another questionable Obama associate is openly gay Stanford law professor Lawrence Lessig, who was listed during the 2008 campaign as being part of Obama's "technology initiative." In April, Lessig showed a video at a Google seminar entitled *Jesus Christ: The Musical* where "Jesus Christ lip-syncs Gloria Gaynor's late '70s disco hit *I Will Survive* during which he strips down to just a diaper, effeminately struts along a city street, and finally gets run over by a speeding bus."

Are three murders taking place within the span of 40 days among members of America's most notorious church—one run by the controversial Rev. Jeremiah Wright—enough to arouse the suspicions of Chicago law enforcement officials and members of the national media? Or, as Larry Sinclair wrote in a May 18 e-mail, was the murder of Donald Young "made to look similar to other recent murders as to make it look as if it were a hate crime" because he had become a political liability? One can only hope that this isn't the beginning of another body count eerily reminiscent of those associated with Bill and Hillary Clinton.

Obama's Globalist Ties Exposed

Originally published: June 30, 2008

 National media outlets were abuzz Friday morning, June 5, with news that Barack Obama and Hillary Clinton had a secret rendezvous the night before, purportedly at the house of California Senator Diane Feinstein. What they failed to mention was that only a few miles away, the most famous clandestine group in the world—the Bilderbergers—were also meeting in Chantilly, Virginia.

Obama's participation in this shadowy confab with Clinton should raise eyebrows because we've all been told ad nauseam that the presumptive Democratic nominee represents "change." But is this statement necessarily true? For starters, Senator Diane Feinstein owns the Beltway mansion in which he supposedly hunkered down with Mrs. Clinton. Feinstein is a member of the Trilateral Commission, Council on Foreign Relations, and frequent Bilderberg attendee in the past. There is also strong evidence brought out in the June 9 & 16, 2008 issue (#23/24) of AMERICAN FREE PRESS that she has profited handsomely from the Iraq War.

But this serendipitous late-night session is only one of many links tying Obama to the New World Order. Suspicions that he was being groomed for a run at the White House became apparent in August 2007—before most Americans even knew who Obama was—when Zbigniew Brzezinski endorsed Obama for president. It should be noted that Obama hadn't even declared that he was running for the Oval Office yet, let alone assembled any type of formal committee.

Brzezinski, of course, is a longtime globalist luminary whose mentor is none other than David Rockefeller. After reading Brzezinski's 1970 book, *Between Two Ages*, which unabashedly advocated a socialist-style world government, Rockefeller recruited Brzezinski to jointly found the Trilateral

Commission with him. Rockefeller then pitched this idea for "trilaterlism" at the 1972 meeting of the Bilderbergs in Belgium.

Another one of Brzezinski's influential books, *The Grand Chessboard*, served as one of the seminal blueprints for events leading up to the 9-11 terrorist attacks, as well as America's current debacle in Iraq. Other documents that advanced this "cause" were Professor Samuel Huntington's *Clash of Civilizations*, the PNAC's *Rebuilding America's Defenses* and Benjamin Netanyahu's *Fighting Terrorism* where he coined the term "War on Terror."

But Brzezinski's fixation with Eurasia goes much deeper. While acting as Jimmy Carter's national security adviser, Brzezinski admitted many years later that he was responsible for establishing America's covert actions that compelled the USSR to invade Afghanistan. He stated, "The secret operation was an excellent idea. It had the effect of drawing the Russians into the Afghan trap . . . the day that the Soviets officially crossed the border, I wrote to President Carter: we now have the opportunity of giving to the USSR its Vietnam War."

This provocation led to bringing about the Soviet Union's collapse, while also ending the Cold War. On the other hand, according to plan, new "enemies" were created—the Taliban, al Qaeda and Osama bin Laden—all of whom were clandestinely funded for years by the CIA and Pakistan's ISI. Over a million men were ultimately killed during the Afghanistan War, in addition to the fact that a perfect Orwellian enemy was created when Muslims were pitted against Christians—all to Israel's obvious benefit because the U.S. would be doing its dirty work for them.

Let there be no doubt that Brzezinski was an integral architect of this "endless war," for he theorized in the mid-1990s that the only way American leaders could justify a prolonged war in the Middle East was via a Pearl Harbor-style external threat. Conveniently enough, he also predicted that "Afghan terrorists" would attack the U.S. (i.e. the 9-11 false flag terror strikes), and that the United States would eventually target Iran for invasion. So far, his crystal ball has been eerily accurate.

Brzezinski's meddling in genocidal wars wasn't limited to the Middle East. He was also an ardent backer of Cambodia's ruthless dictator Pol Pot, whose Khmer Rouge slaughtered over two-million people and buried them in mass graves. When asked about supplying direct military aid to these killers, Brzezinski acknowledged, "I encouraged the Chinese to support Pol

Pot. . . . Pol Pot was an abomination. We could never support him, but China could."

Considering his monstrous motives and globalist philosophy, Barack Obama still selected Brzezinski to be his foreign policy "advisor" during his campaign. While giving a policy speech on the Iraq War in September 2007, Obama said that Brzezinski was "one of our most outstanding scholars and thinkers," and that he was "someone I have learned an immense amount from."

Another clue that Obama has accepted the tenets of a one-world government is his sponsorship of the "Global Poverty Act" where the United Nations would directly tax American citizens. He has also selected Susan Rice—a member of the CFR, Trilateral Commission and Brookings Institute—to be another foreign policy adviser; while Anthony Lake is also a member of his inner circle. Lake is a notable Henry Kissinger protégé, Bill Clinton's former national security adviser, as well as a man who was instrumental in making policy decisions leading up to the atrocious murder of over 800,000 Rwandans—another inexcusable genocide.

Last but not least, we should all hark back to the seminal event that placed Barack Obama on the national stage. It occurred in 2004 at the Democratic National Convention, where Obama—a recently elected unknown freshman senator from Illinois—delivered a charismatic keynote speech which electrified the audience. Who was the man responsible for handpicking Obama; the man who literally "made" him, so to speak? It was none other than Yale Skull & Bonesman John Kerry, who ran against fellow Skull & Bonesman George W. Bush in 2004. Is this the kind of "change" to which Barack Obama keeps referring?

Robert Bennett

Bill Clinton

Non-partisan group

HILLARY CLINTON AND BARACK OBAMA   STRINGER/GETTY IMAGES

Barack Obama & Hillary Clinton: Two Consummate Insiders Cut From The Same Globalist Cloth

Originally published: August 4, 2008

109,175,175. That's how much money Bill and Hillary Clinton earned from 2000 to 2007. Yet after the 2008 Democratic primaries, Mrs. Clinton is now seeking assistance in repaying her $23 million campaign debt. Oddly enough, when Steve Forbes and Mitt Romney—both wealthy men—ran for the presidency, neither sought help in covering their expenses. Rather, they took the money from their own pockets and paid what was owed.

But not Hillary Clinton. Similar to most politicians in D.C. who have become accustomed to—even *addicted* to—a culture of governmental welfare subsidies that supports their lavish lifestyles, Mrs. Clinton is no different. Instead of taking personal responsibility for her vast expenditures, she now expects Barack Obama, the Democratic Party and everyday citizens to get her out of the red.

But here's the catch. Of the $23 million she still owes, $11 million is owed to herself in the form of personal loans. The reason Hillary is so intent on recouping this money is that, according to campaign finance laws, if she doesn't pay off this debt by the Democratic National Convention on August 25, the loans will be re-categorized as contributions and Hillary will lose all $11 million of her own personal assets. Now can you tell why she's so desperate?

Hillary isn't concerned with anyone else's debt, however, as can be witnessed by her reaction to Jo Liston of Harlington, Texas, who was contracted to provide van and minibus services during the primaries. The bill was $650, yet after sending numerous invoices, this small business owner has received nothing but a cold shoulder and isn't sure if she'll ever get paid. Such behavior is typical of Bill and Hillary Clinton, who've made a career out of running roughshod over everyone in their path, then leaving the wreckage behind.

What we're talking about is cold, calculated opportunism and Machiavellian-like career advancement. Now that Barack Obama has been recruited to cajole money from his supporters to help Hillary, an even more important story has emerged. Being the consummate operative, Hillary is once again promoting the New World Order's agenda by opening the doors of her inner circle to Obama and helping him raise large amounts of cash.

Despite a supposed "war" that's been played out in the media, have Obama and Hillary been working hand-in-hand all along to ensure a Democratic victory this fall? First, consider that their primary battle was the longest in history, with its length allowing Obama to not only amass a daunting war chest for his race against John McCain, but also garnering millions of new left-leaning voters registered in all 50 states—oftentimes surpassing Republicans, as they did in Pennsylvania.

Of course the uninitiated in each camp may not like each other, and the well-publicized animosity between Hillary and Barack provides great fodder to perpetuate the illusion that real democracy is at work in America. But remember: to reach such a prominent level on the national stage, one must be an insider who is willing to sell his soul to play the game. Obama, Hillary and McCain have all done so; as did George W. Bush, John Kerry, Al Gore, Bill Clinton and many others before them. The Bushes and Clintons have been on the same team for decades working in unison, and now it seems the door has been opened to Barack Obama.

Take, for example, two glitzy New York City fundraisers jointly attended by Hillary and Obama on July 10-11 that added nearly $15 million to the presumptive Democratic nominee's coffers. Jewish socialites Barbaralee Diamonstein and Carl Spielvogel—two of the top ten Clinton contributors since the 1980s—organized one of these functions. Both were repaid handsomely and received sleepover privileges in the White House Lincoln Bedroom during Bill Clinton's tenure as president. Spielvogel was also appointed ambassador to Slovakia by Clinton, and has been a staunch advocate of globalism since the early 1970s.

Also in attendance at this $33,100 per plate event held at the Loews Regency Hotel was none other than Vernon Jordan, Mrs. Clinton's most influential handler for over thirty years. A long-time Bilderberg member, Jordan has opened many doors for both Clintons and helped them escape scandals for decades. Now, via Hillary, he has definitely made the acquaintance of Barack Obama, who touts his own list of NWO luminaries, including Zbigniew Brzezinski.

As the presidential election unfolds this fall, never forget that what you're seeing is a political drama that has been well crafted and finely orchestrated by the world's most powerful people. Barack Obama is the latest initiate, but his naivete and greenhorn status are still clearly visible, as was recently shown when he forgot to mention that his supporters should contribute money to help retire his opponent's campaign debt. That's why a seasoned veteran like Hillary Clinton is required on the scene. She needs to keep an eye on the global elite's latest prize—Barack Obama—the same way she did three decades earlier with her husband.

Naturally, pundits from all the major media outlets will keep teasing you with stories about Jesse Jackson calling Barack Obama a "nigger" and wanting to castrate him, but keep in mind that much more is going on behind the scenes. Covering the above-mentioned Loews Regency gala, *Newsweek's* Andrew Romano reported that Hillary Clinton called her relationship with Obama, "one of those Ginger Rogers-Fred Astaire things." In return, Obama strayed from his prepared text and raised some eyebrows when he declared, "We will change the country and change the world, and you will give Senator Hillary Clinton and Barack Obama a chance to transform America once again."

There has always been an unseen hand ruling the presidency. Colonel Edward House pulled Woodrow Wilson's strings and got the U.S. into World War I, while Lyndon Johnson radically changed American policy after John Kennedy was assassinated. Likewise, George Bush Sr. controlled all the illegal operations during Ronald Reagan's two terms, and it's safe to say that Dick Cheney played a significant role in the 9-11 terrorist attacks. As I pointed out in my latest trilogy on the Clintons, Hillary was actually more of a hands-on governor of Arkansas and president of the United States than was her husband. In regard to Barack Obama, has this been Mrs. Clinton's role all along—to be one of the hidden powers behind the throne?

GERMAN NEWSPAPERS ANNOUNCE THE OBAMA VICTORY.

JOHN MACDOUGALL/AFP/GETTY IMAGES

Barack's Berlin Speech Exposes Wolf in Sheep's Clothing

Originally published: August 11, 2008

Standing in front of Berlin's Victory Column on July 24, 2008, Barack Obama delivered one of the most New World Order-laden speeches in the history of American politics. Although most people unfamiliar with the global elite's symbolism probably didn't realize it, Obama laced his oratory with enough doublespeak and hot button terminology to make his hidden masters smile with delight.

Beginning by calling himself a "citizen of the world," Obama told the crowd of 200,000, "People of the world, do your duty." Urging sacrifice, he proclaimed that all of us should stand up against the evils of our world. But Obama didn't mean evils such as globalism, villainous moneylenders, government leaders who order false-flag terrorist attacks, or corrupt taxation. Instead, he was referring to climate change and how we should subject ourselves to a blatant form of eco-communist legislation, with the U.S. ultimately being further taxed and regulated by global institutions such as those appropriated by Al Gore.

To reach this end, he stated, "Partnership and cooperation among nations is not a choice. It is the one way, the only way, to advance our common humanity." Amid this advocacy for unbridled collectivism was a call to "build new bridges across the globe" because "now is the time to join together, through constant cooperation, strong institutions, shared sacrifices, and a global commitment to progress." The most obvious question is: to what type of "strong institutions" was he referring?

An answer can be found in Obama placing the importance of our "planet" over personal freedom and national sovereignty by saying that we

BUSINESS AS USUAL

All four nominees being considered to fill the post of Treasury Department Secretary are Jewish: Robert Rubin (shown above), Lawrence Summers and Paul Volcker. Coincidentally, the last three Federal Reserve chairmen have also been Jewish, controlling this privately owned institution since 1979. Barack Obama's vice president, Joseph Biden, recently raised eyebrows when he told Rabbi Mark S. Golub of *Shalom TV*, "I am a Zionist. You don't have to be a Jew to be a Zionist." He also rationalized during this same interview that Israeli spy Jonathan Pollard "deserves leniency." Meanwhile, John Podesta, a Jewish former Clintonista who served as deputy chief of staff, spearheads Obama's transition team. At his side is Pete Rouse, described by the *Washington Post* as "the Outsider's Insider, a fixer steeped in the ways of Washington." It just shows that the more things change, the more they stay the same.

must renew the goals of the world. To do so, he unabashedly promoted a socialist-style agenda. "We must build on the wealth that open markets have created and share its benefits more equitably." Shared prosperity, of course, is the cornerstone of Marxist ideology, and the end result doesn't make everyday people any freer or more sovereign as individuals. Rather, they're turned into undifferentiated, uninspired cogs-in-the-wheel—eventually consumed and defeated by the state.

Not surprisingly, when Obama wants us to forge trade that rewards the "many," it harks back to his association with black liberation theologian Rev. Jeremiah Wright, who makes no bones whatsoever about being a Marxist. Also, considering Obama's sponsorship of the "Global Poverty Act" where the U.S. would be directly taxed by the United Nations, it is almost as if the ghost of Karl Marx himself was pleading, "Workers of the world unite" under the flag of collectivism.

The title of Obama's speech says it all: "A World That Stands as One." Those of us who shudder at the thought of such undisguised globalist rhetoric will be even more alarmed when we're reminded of a demand Michelle Obama made earlier in 2008. "Barack will never allow you to go back to your lives as usual."

Is this the "change" we're been hearing so much about since the presidential race began in January 2008? An even eerier moment came at the conclusion of Obama's speech where he declared, "I know my country has not perfected itself." Although seemingly tame on the surface, if one examines the symbolic message of our Great Seal on the back of every dollar bill, they'd understand that the New World Order's ultimate goal is to "perfect" its totalitarian control by placing a capstone on top of its pyramid. This "perfection" will entail even more losses of liberty than was already introduced by George W. Bush under the Patriot Act, Bill Clinton, George Bush, Sr., and a long list of presidents preceding them, including Woodrow Wilson and FDR.

Be wary of change, especially when it masquerades as a wolf wearing the sheep's clothing of charisma and hope.

Top, members of the Weather Underground, a radical group bent on overthrowing the government of the United States, protest the Vietnam War in Chicago in 1969. After the group disbanded, several members offered their services to radical black nationalists. **Left,** a mugshot of William Ayers after his arrest by Chicago police. Ayers remains unrepentant to this day for the misery he caused innocent Americans. William Ayers' reign of terror ended in 1970 when three fellow Weathermen blew themselves up with a bomb filled with nails **(lower right).** Ayers's cohorts had planned to detonate the bomb at a social dance at Fort Dix, N.J., hoping to kill as many innocent Americans as possible.

Obama's Disturbing Connection To Terrorist William Ayers

Originally published: September 15, 2008

William Ayers was one of the most notorious domestic terrorists in this nation's history. His group—the Weather Underground—bombed New York City police headquarters in 1970, the Capitol Building in 1971 and the Pentagon in 1972. On September 11, 2001 while Americans watched in horror as our nation was attacked, William Ayers told *The New York Times*, "I don't regret setting bombs. I feel we didn't do enough."

Ayers would be relegated to nothing more than a footnote to the radical '60s Left if it weren't for the fact that when Barack Obama announced his candidacy for the Illinois Senate in 1995, he did it at William Ayers' house.

In addition to the previously listed acts of violence, this is the same William Ayers who was involved in bombing courthouses, banks, police barracks, a National Guard outpost, and other government buildings. The Weathermen also blew up a statue (on two different occasions) in Chicago's Haymarket Square, broke LSD guru Timothy Leary out of prison and set off a pipe bomb in San Francisco that killed one police officer, while blinding another. They also advocated the attack of innocent civilians, vandalism and arson to get their message across. In all, the Weather Underground engaged in dozens of these attacks across the U.S. in the early 1970s.

His reign of terror ended when a bomb they were constructing in Greenwich Village exploded, killing three of his fellow Weathermen. The device, packed with boxes of carpenter nails to inflict maximum damage, was meant for a dance hall attended by soldiers and their dates at Fort Dix. As David Farber of *The Chicago Tribune* wrote, "It almost surely was intended to kill many people."

An ad campaign sponsored by the American Issues Project in the summer of 2008 asked "Why would Barack Obama 'be friends with someone who bombed the Capitol and is proud of it'?"

After Obama kicked off his senatorial bid at William Ayers's house, he also served with him for three years as a board member on the Woods Fund, a non-profit organization. Further, Obama also appeared with Ayers on two academic panels—the latest taking place in 2002. Both men are also linked to the University of Illinois in Chicago where Ayers teaches, and only live a few blocks from each other. Lastly, Ayers contributed $200 to Obama's state senatorial campaign in 2001.

As is customary, Obama downplays his relationship to Ayers, just as he did with the flamboyant preacher whose church he attended for twenty years—Rev. Jeremiah Wright. Oddly enough, the similarities between Ayers and the Marxist, black nationalist Wright are striking. In 1995, Ayers stated, "Maybe I'm the last Communist who is willing to admit it. The ethics of Communism still appeal to me." Similarly, the Weather Underground's mission statement reveals that they sought to create a "white fighting force to be allied with the black liberation movement." To augment their Marxist links, the Weathermen bombed the Pentagon in 1972 on Ho Chi Minh's birthday, using what they called "an American Red Army."

Ayers's extremism also extends to his wife, fellow Weather Underground member Bernadine Dohrn, who was once listed on the FBI's Ten Most Wanted List. Dohrn is so radical that she made the following comments after Charles Manson's Helter Skelter slayings. "Dig it. First they killed those pigs, then they ate dinner in the same room with them. They even shoved a fork into the victim's stomach. Wild!" Equally as disturbing, reminiscent of Rev. Wright who refers to our nation as the "U.S. KKK of A.," Dohrn calls our country "AmeriKKKa."

Ayers' philosophy is no different. In the 1970s, he advised his followers, "Kill all the rich people. Break up their cars and apartments. Bring the revolution home. Kill your parents. That's where it's really at."

Obama apologists will dismiss these sentiments as merely the follies of a misguided youth. But in his 2001 book, *Fugitive Days*, Ayers said of America, "What a country. It makes me want to puke." Similarly, when asked if

WILLIAM AYERS: Modern-day photograph of aging former terrorist.

he'd ever again consider bombing targets in the U.S., he responded, "I can't imagine entirely dismissing the possibility."

Today, William Ayers has no regrets about his terrorist past; and according to University of Chicago law professor Cass Sunstein, Ayers "refuses to disavow what he did." This isn't surprising, especially when Ayers boasted in his 2001 book, "Everything was absolutely ideal on the day I bombed the Pentagon . . . . There's something about a good bomb." Of the 300+ million people living in America, why would Barack Obama announce his candidacy for the Illinois Senate in the home of William Ayers, and why would he continue his relationship with him into the future? That might be the biggest Obama bomb of all.

Obama 'Assassination Plot' Smells Like a Set-Up

Originally published: November 10, 2008

On Monday, October 27, 2008, two teenagers described as "neo-nazi skinheads" by the media were apprehended in Tennessee after allegedly planning to kill presidential candidate Barack Obama. This case followed the arrest of three methamphetamine-addicted Denver men in August who were involved in a "half-baked plot" to assassinate Obama. The press portrayed these individuals as being "white supremacists" and "Aryans."

Although neither scenario had any credible possibility of being carried out, a larger question must be asked. Is a foundation being laid to pin some sort of high-profile crime on nationalists, populists, patriots, 9-11 truthers or so-called conspiracy theorists? Of course there is a precedent for such tactics. In 1995, Timothy McVeigh and his cohorts at Elohim City were targeted as the masterminds of OKC, even though reams of evidence have surfaced pointing to a pre-planned controlled demolition involving the FBI, CIA and ATF. Led by the Southern Poverty Law Center and a complicit mainstream media, the blowback from this tragic event pointed an accusatory finger at conservative talk radio, the *Spotlight* newspaper, and a growing militia movement. All suffered serious consequences as a result of this despicable act of false-flag terrorism.

Now, with a Democratic president and a Democratically controlled Congress, are steps being taken to repeat the above story line? In the October 27 arrests, two deluded teenagers—Daniel Cowart and Paul Schlesselman—purportedly wanted to kill 88 Tennessee high school students, then decapitate 14 other blacks. Following this rampage, they then intended to "drive their vehicle as fast as they could toward [Barack] Obama, shooting

DANIEL DOWART: Is this the "mastermind" behind the "plot" to kill Obama?

at him from the windows. Both individuals stated they would dress in all white tuxedos and wear top hats during the assassination attempt."

Their blueprint for murder was obviously preposterous, especially since Obama wasn't even going to be in Tennessee. Authorities described the plot as not being "very advanced or sophisticated," and that "it does not appear to have moved to an advanced stage." Still, reports highlight the seeming symbolic significance of the numbers used in this hare-brained scheme. "88" is supposed to represent "Heil Hitler" (the eighth letter of the alphabet), while "14" reportedly referred to the number of words in a popular "white supremacy" motto ("We must secure the existence of our people and a future for white children").

There was zero possibility that the Tennessee or Denver contingents could have realistically assassinated Obama, yet news reports are alleging that these groups were targeting the "Zionist-occupied government," and are using other such highly charged buzzwords. Is this how the stage is being set for a repeat of OKC 1995, with the scapegoats being members of the patriot movement? The picture gets even more frightening when we consider Vice President Joseph Biden's October 19, 2008, remarks when he spoke of a "manufactured crisis" being used to test Barack Obama. If such a scenario does emerge, it would surely lead to a frenzy of new congressional legislation, with gun rights, the Fairness Doctrine and our Constitution being squarely in the crosshairs.

WHITE HOUSE CHIEF OF STAFF RAHM EMANUEL

RAHM EMANUEL:
Obama's Choice for Chief of Staff Has Long Pro-Zionist History

Originally published: November 24, 2008

More sinister than Karl Rove and potentially deadlier than Darth Cheney, his name is Rahm Emanuel, and he was appointed chief of staff in Obama's new Cabinet. This first official act should send waves of alarm through people because Barack Obama promised change, but what we're getting is the exact same cabal that brought us 9-11 and endless war in the Mideast. Initial media reports described Emanuel as a vulgar, Chicago-based enforcer who had an aggressive, in-your-face pit bull style. Others painted him as a partisan D.C. insider with strong ties to Nancy Pelosi. Although these labels seem harsh, the reality is far worse. Rahm Emanuel, nicknamed "Rahmbo," is a pro-Israel Orthodox Jew who was educated in a Talmudic *yeshiva* and served as a volunteer in the IDF (Israeli Defense Force). Those familiar with the 9-11 terrorist attacks know that the IDF was instrumental in training the dancing Israelis who—from a rooftop in Weehawken, New Jersey—had the foreknowledge to videotape both WTC towers being struck by kamikaze jetliners, then celebrate afterward.

Mentored by members of Chicago's corrupt party machine like convicted Congressman Dan Rostenkowski, Emanuel gravitated to Washington in 1991 after becoming Bill Clinton's campaign finance committee director. His star rose even higher when he served as one of the primary NAFTA architects and pushed strict anti-gun legislation. After leaving his post as a policy aide for the Clintons, he used his influence as an investment banker to rake in millions during the late 1990s. With this money, Emanuel won a congressional seat in 2002, became the fourth ranking House Democrat by 2006, and is now the most powerful member of Obama's executive office team.

FAMILY HISTORY OF VIOLENCE

If the story ended there, it would be bad enough. What truly makes Emanuel dangerous is that his Israeli-born father Benjamin was an integral member of the Zionist terror group known as Irgun during the 1940s. Along with another notorious terror outfit—the Stern Gang—Irgun bombed Jerusalem's King David Hotel in 1946 where 96 people were killed, while also instigating the 1948 Deir Yassin Massacre.   •

Rahm Emanuel is the son of a terrorist who directly plotted the assassination of Count Bernadotte, a Swedish diplomat and United Nations envoy who tried to broker peace in Palestine. But Irgun didn't seek treaties. They instead sought racial cleansing and genocide. According to Elisabeth Bumiller in *The New York Times*, Benjamin Emanuel passed secret codes to Shin Bet bomber and future Prime Minister Menachem Begin. These very same Jewish terrorists eventually became the recognized Israeli government in 1948, as well as predecessors to Benjamin Netanyahu's right-wing Likud Party.

OBAMA'S SVENGALI

Rahm Emanuel likes to brag about his role in discovering Barack Obama. "Six years ago, people on the North Side of Chicago took a bet on a young kid," reporter D.H. Williams writes of their symbiotic relationship. "Rahm and Barack have a deep history together in Chicago politics. Emanuel has been instrumental in the rise of Barack Obama from neophyte senator to the next president of the United States. Getting virtually no media attention, Rahm Emanuel has been by Obama's side during most of the last two years on the campaign trail." If Karl Rove was George W. Bush's architect, the same can be said of the Emanuel connection. When Obama bowed and groveled at the American Israel Public Affairs Committee (AIPAC) convention on June 4, 2008, it was Emanuel who escorted him to meet the executive board afterward.

To put this situation into perspective, Rabbi Dov Zakheim acted as the invisible mastermind of 9-11. Likewise, Emanuel has been the operative who, according to *The Chicago Tribune*, "remade the Democratic Party in his own image." Illinois representative Ray LaHood seconded this notion. "He legitimately can be called the golden boy of the Democratic Party today. He recruited the right candidates, found the money and funded them, and provided issues for them. Rahm did what no one else could do."

Worst of all, Emanuel is a rampant warmonger who takes his cues from the neo-cons. In his book *The Plan: Big Ideas for America*, he wrote, "We need to expand the U.S. Army by 100,000 more troops." What will America's next target be under an Obama presidency? Sources close to Emanuel say that he has a "Zionist obsession with Iran."

To get a final idea of what we're dealing with, consider this quote from American war journalist Pat Dollard:

> Let me tell you right now, no exaggeration: Rahm Emanuel is the devil. He is literally a Goebbels, a Mengele, a perfect Cromwell who would, without the faintest evidence of hesitation washing across his face for even a trillisecond, order and even personally execute each and every human being he or Obama perceived to be an enemy of the regime. And if you ever personally offended him, and he had the opportunity to kill you, he would probably do it by starting with your children as you were made to watch. He is a bad guy.

Some researchers have gone so far as to claim that Emanuel was the notorious "Mega" spy deep inside the Clinton administration that passed top-secret documents about Iran on to the Israeli government, causing a great deal of chaos among our various intelligence agencies. Be very wary of this man. Like the "Prince of Darkness" Richard Perle and Michael Chertoff before him (both of whom hold dual U.S.-Israeli citizenships), it may well be proven that his loyalties rest more with a fabricated little state in the Middle East than they do with the United States.

Obama Inner Circle Filled With CFR, Trilats, Bilderbergers

Originally published: December 22, 2008

For two years, Americans heard an unrelenting mantra of "change" emanating from the campaign trail. But when Barack Obama formed his cabinet, we saw more deeply entrenched insiders appointed than by any administration that has ever preceded it. Below is an overview of Obama's top thirteen selections to date. When considering their collective histories, a trend becomes abundantly clear, proving that the more things change, the more they stay the same.

TIMOTHY GEITHNER—TREASURY SECRETARY

Jewish, Bilderberg, senior fellow Council on Foreign Relations, Trilateral Commission, president & CEO of Federal Reserve Bank of New York, Director of Policy Development for International Monetary Fund, member Group of Thirty (G30), employed at Kissinger & Associates, architect of the recent financial bailouts during the Bush administration, mentored by Lawrence Summers and Robert Rubin.

PAUL VOLCKER—ECONOMIC RECOVERY ADVISORY BOARD

Jewish, Bilderberg, Council on Foreign Relations, North American chairman of Trilateral Commission, Federal Reserve chairman during Carter and Reagan administrations, president of Federal Reserve Bank of New York, G30 member, chairman Rothschild Wolfensohn Company, key figure in the collapse of the gold standard during the Nixon administration, longtime associate of the Rockefeller family.

TIMOTHY GEITHNER   HILLARY CLINTON   JOSEPH BIDEN   TOM DASCHLE

RAHM EMANUEL—CHIEF OF STAFF

Jewish, member of Israeli Defense Force, Zionist, U.S. senator, Board of Directors for Freddie Mac, member of Bill Clinton's finance campaign committee, made $16.2 million during two years as an investment banker for Wasserstein Perella; his father was a member of the infamous Israeli Irgun terrorist group.

LAWRENCE SUMMERS—NATIONAL ECONOMIC COUNCIL

Jewish, Bilderberg, Council on Foreign Relations, Trilateral Commission, treasury secretary during Clinton administration, chief economist at World Bank, former president of Harvard University, Brookings Institute board member, huge proponent of globalization while working for the IMF, protégé of David Rockefeller, mentored by Robert Rubin.

DAVID AXELROD—SENIOR ADVISOR

Jewish, political consultant whose past clients include Hillary Clinton, John Edwards and Christopher Dodd, main Obama fixer in the William Ayers and Rev. Wright scandals.

HILLARY CLINTON—SECRETARY OF STATE

Bilderberg, Council on Foreign Relations, Trilateral Commission, clandestine CIA asset used to infiltrate the anti-war movement at Yale University and the Watergate hearings, senior partner at the Rose Law Firm, key figure in the Mena drug trafficking affair with George Bush Sr. and others in his administration, architect of the Waco disaster, implicated in the murder/cover-up of Vince Foster and Ron Brown (among others).

JANET NAPOLITANO   JAMES L JONES   ERIC HOLDER   SUSAN RICE

JOSEPH BIDEN—VICE PRESIDENT

Bilderberg, chairman of the Council on Foreign Relations, U.S. Senator since 1972, chairman of the Senate Judiciary Committee, chairman of the U.S. Senate Committee on Foreign Relations, strong Zionist sympathizer who recently told Rabbi Mark S. Golub of *Shalom TV*, "I am a Zionist. You don't have to be a Jew to be a Zionist."

BILL RICHARDSON—COMMERCE SECRETARY

Bilderberg, Council on Foreign Relations, U.S. congressman, chairman of the Democratic National Convention in 2004, employee of Kissinger Associates, UN ambassador, governor of New Mexico, energy secretary, major player in the Lewinsky cover-up with Bilderberg luminary Vernon Jordan.

ROBERT GATES—DEFENSE SECRETARY

Bilderberg, Council on Foreign Relations, former CIA director, defense secretary under George W. Bush, co-chaired CFR task force with Zbigniew Brzezinski, knee-deep in the Iran-Contra scandal, named in a 1999 class action lawsuit pertaining to the Mena drug trafficking affair.

TOM DASCHLE—HEALTH SECRETARY (WITHDREW FROM CONSIDERATION)

Bilderberg, Council on Foreign Relations, Senate majority leader, Citibank lackey, mentored by Robert Rubin.

ERIC HOLDER—ATTORNEY GENERAL

Key person in the pardon of Jewish racketeer Marc Rich, deputy attorney general under Janet Reno, facilitated the pardon of 16 Puerto Rican FALN terrorists under Bill Clinton.

JANET NAPOLITANO—HOMELAND SECURITY DIRECTOR

Council on Foreign Relations, Arizona governor, attorney for Anita Hill during the Clarence Thomas hearings, U.S. attorney during the Clinton administration, instrumental in the OKC cover-up where she declared, "We'll pursue every bit of evidence and every lead," described as another Janet Reno, soft on illegal immigration (i.e. pro-amnesty and drivers licenses to illegals).

GENERAL JAMES L. JONES—NATIONAL SECURITY ADVISOR

Bilderberg, Trilateral Commission, European Supreme Allied Commander, special envoy for Middle-East Security during Bush administration, Board of Directors for Chevron and Boeing, NATO Commander, member of Brent Scowcroft's Institute for International Affairs along with Zbigniew Brzezinski, Bobby Ray Inman, Henry Kissinger and former CIA Director John Deutch.

SUSAN RICE—UN AMBASSADOR

Council on Foreign Relations, Rhodes Scholar, campaign foreign policy advisor to John Kerry and Michael Dukakis, member of Bill Clinton's National Security Council and assistant secretary of state to Africa, member of the Brookings Institute (funded by the Ford Foundation and the Rockefellers), and member of the Aspen Strategy Group (teeming with Bilderberg insiders such as Richard Armitage, Brent Scowcroft and Madeleine Albright).

It should be noted that in regard to key foreign policy advisers, all three of Obama's selections either initially supported the Iraq War, or do at this time. On the economic front, each appointee maintains a close relationship with the Jewish triad of Ben Bernanke, Robert Rubin and Alan Greenspan; as well as bailout engineer Henry Paulson. Lastly, Barack Obama himself is a Council on Foreign Relations member, has strong ties to Zbigniew Brzezinski and participated in a clandestine meeting with Hillary Clinton at Bilderberg member Diane Feinstein's house at the time when 2008 Bilderberg members were congregating only a few miles away. During the last three administrations, we've gone from Bill Clinton's Arkansas Dixie Mafia to George W. Bush's Texas oil cabal, and now to Barack Obama's Chicago gangsters. So much for change.

Chicago Shakedown: How Close is Obama?

Originally published: January 26, 2008

"It's a f—-ing valuable thing, and it's golden. I'm just not giving it up for f—-ing nothing." This eloquent phrasing was how Illinois Gov. Rod Blagojevich described the potential sale of a Senate seat left vacant by Barack Obama. Not only did he seek upwards of a million dollars for this highly prized position, the governor also wanted either a spot in Obama's Cabinet, a lucrative union job or access as a lobbyist for his wife.

U.S. Attorney Patrick Fitzgerald revealed these shady deals (and others) after Blagojevich's office was bugged and his phones tapped. During a December 9 press conference, Fitzgerald described his reaction to Chicago's political machine. "This is a sad day for government. It's a very sad day for Illinois government. Gov. Blagojevich has taken us to a truly new low . . . this conduct would make Lincoln roll over in his grave."

Selling Obama's Senate seat wasn't the only element of this politically corrupt crime spree. Other pay-to-play schemes devised by Blagojevich included kickbacks for a tollway project, children's hospital and legislation involving a horse racing track. Even more blatant was his strong-arming of *The Chicago Tribune*, who had called for Blagojevich's impeachment in several critical articles. In response, the governor threatened to impede one of their business deals unless several editors were dismissed. In his own words, Blagojevich demanded, "Fire all those f---ing people. Get them the f--k out of there."

The governor's wife even entered the fray. Described as a domineering, Lady Macbeth-style prima donna, she too stood to benefit from their illegal endeavors. At one point, her husband was heard arranging on her behalf "a well-paid post on a corporate board with around $150,000 a year that would help alleviate the family's financial stress." She was also recorded urging the governor to impede *The Chicago Tribune's* sale of Wrigley Field, which its parent company owns. "Hold up that f---ing Cubs [deal]. F--k them." A real classy couple, don't you think?

OBAMA'S CHIEF-OF-STAFF

Dual U.S.-Israeli citizen Rahm Emanuel was put in place to be Obama's pit bull dirty tricks operator. His role in this scandal dates back to 2002 when he filled Gov. Blagojevich's congressional seat. Now, reports filtering out of Chicago suggest that Emanuel met with the governor on multiple occasions, and that their conversations were more than likely recorded during FBI stings. Most sources predict that even before a grand jury convenes, someone searching for leniency will flip and start spilling the beans. If this happens, Emanuel's role becomes crucial, especially when it's already known that he compiled "a list of [senatorial] candidates that would be acceptable to President-elect Barack Obama."

THE JACKSON CONNECTION

Another bombshell was dropped in this case when U.S. attorneys disclosed on October 31 that Blagojevich was taped telling his associates, "We were approached with 'pay to play'. He'd raise me 500 grand. An emissary came. Then the other guy would raise a million if I made him (candidate 5) Senator." The governor continued, stating, "He might be able to cut a deal with Senate candidate 5 that provided something tangible up front."

Candidate 5 was Jesse Jackson, Jr., and on December 11 he gave an impassioned speech denying any wrongdoing. His pleas were difficult to swallow, however, considering that his father—the "Reverend"—is one of the most notorious shakedown artists in American history. Described by various writers as a race hustler, a conniving con man and a professional extortionist, Jackson has made a lucrative career of blackmailing companies so that they bow to his "racial protection racket."

Some of his most high-profile victims include Coca-Cola, Kentucky Fried Chicken, Burger King, Anheuser-Busch and CBS. By using strong-arm tactics to race-bait these entities, he first makes certain demands, and

ERIC HOLDER AND PATRICK FITZGERALD

if they're not met, he organizes groups like Operation PUSH to boycott these organizations. With a complicit media in tow, they continue their public pressure until a payoff is delivered. As author Kenneth Timmerman wrote in *Shakedown*, Jackson's intimidation and coercion have "enriched his family, steered billions of business to his friends and launched a political dynasty."

Jackson has been drowning America with "white guilt" for the past three decades, but whenever his own indiscretions are exposed, he cries "racism" to divert attention. For example, what are we to make of a supposed spiritual leader who commits adultery with his employee, fathers her illegitimate love child, then uses $40,000 of tax-exempt company funds as hush money to keep her quiet? Timmerman also addresses how Jackson "defrauded the government of millions of dollars in federal grants," while Paul Campos of *The Rocky Mountain News* questions how the preacher could conceivably "bill the charities he controls $614,000 for travel expenses" in 2000?

WILL OBAMA BE TARGETED?

Whereas Jesse Jackson's crimes include fraud, racketeering and tax evasion, it seems more than a little coincidental that his son—now vying for this cherished Senate seat—was also a member of Barack Obama's presidential campaign team. In addition, Toby Harnden of the UK's *Telegraph* reports that Michelle Obama "has close personal links to the Jackson family." With Rahm Emanuel's connection to this scandal firmly established, it's also known that Obama's convicted slumlord pal, Tony Rezko, gave prosecutors reams of information to build their case against Blagojevich. Rezko also pumped millions of dollars into the previous campaigns of Obama and Blagojevich, and hosted the governor's first post-election bash at his mansion.

Further, according to security analyst Larry Johnson, Obama's primary fixer and chief strategist, David Axelrod, "has close ties with Blagojevich and ran his first campaign for the House." Axelrod also initially told *Fox News* that Obama did speak with the governor about his former Senate seat; then retracted this statement after the scandal broke. The preferred candidate in question was Valerie Jarrett, a Chicago insider who once hired Michelle Obama and conveniently enough happens to be one of Obama's longest serving senior advisers.

Is a mini-Watergate brewing? Author Joan Swirsky thinks so, especially after noting how "the arrested governor and president-elect have been connected at the hip for decades." The biggest remaining variable is how close the storm's center will get to Barack Obama, and what steps his handlers take to deal with it.

Has Obama heard the last of Rod Blagojevich? Check back in 2012.

Brazen Illinois Governor Sealed His Fate When He Threatened Bank of America

Originally published: February 16, 2008

C hinese leaders have an old saying: Kill one; silence a thousand. Last week, America's banking godfathers and Chicago's notorious political Mob applied the same adage to Gov. Rod Blagojevich. He wasn't actually slain, but on January 29, 2009 Illinois legislators impeached him in what became nothing less than a media firestorm-public lynching.

Did Blagojevich deserve his comeuppance? Absolutely. His shakedown schemes, bribery attempts and general aura of corruption represent everything that is wrong with our system today. But pundits have overlooked the larger implications of this scandal. Specifically, those who placed Barack Obama in the White House sent a very clear message—don't mess with the ruling elite in this country or you'll take a very unceremonious fall. Since Gov. Blagojevich was already dirty and—more importantly—expendable, he became a scapegoat who served as an example for anyone else that considered pulling back the veil and exposing those who are behind the biggest money racket this nation has ever seen (i.e. billion dollar bailouts and "stimulus" packages).

Blagojevich initially crossed his party bosses by trying to orchestrate an appointment for Obama's recently vacated Senate seat that ran contrary to their wishes. Rather than selecting Valerie Jarrett, co-chair of Obama's transition team and former director of Chicago's Federal Reserve Bank, he instead hinted at Attorney General Lisa Madigan. Blagojevich's self-interests were apparent because Madigan was a political rival who posed a serious challenge to his reelection in 2010. By sending her to the nation's capital, his campaign would have clear sailing the following year.

In addition, Obama's handlers refused to engage in a "pay-to-play" arrangement for this prized seat. Upon hearing that no "quid pro quo" kickback money would be forthcoming, Blagojevich erupted (while being recorded), "If they're not willing to give me anything except appreciation, f--- them."

Blagojevich's alleged desire to sell this seat wasn't the only factor in his downfall. According to former San Francisco Mayor Willie Brown, "Apparently, Obama's people weren't happy about the idea of Madigan coming to Washington, and there were some pretty heated conversations between Blagojevich and Obama Chief of Staff Rahm Emanuel, which I understand will burn your ears off."

This point of contention between the two camps led to another potential pratfall. Obama's primary Zionist pit bull enforcer—Rahm Emanuel—was now implicated in the scandal.

To eliminate this problem, *Think Progress* reported on December 9, 2008 that, "Rahm Emanuel may have tipped off federal investigators that Gov. Blagojevich was engaging in corrupt acts" and that he "might have been responsible for causing federal investigators to act quickly to apprehend Blagojevich." It was Emanuel who presented a list of candidates that would be acceptable to Obama. But once Blagojevich bucked that decision, officers arrived at his home on December 9, 2008 and carted him away in handcuffs.

An even more monumental event took place just one day prior to this arrest. Bank of America refused to issue any more credit to a Chicago-based company named Republic Windows & Doors, which subsequently was forced to shut down and lay off over 200 union employees. But when Bank of America received billions in bailout money and wouldn't restore credit to this company, they staged a sit-in. In turn, Blagojevich took their side and brazenly announced, "We, the State of Illinois, will suspend doing any business with Bank of America." This boycott meant that hundreds of millions of dollars would be withheld from one of this country's top three financial institutions.

Although mainstream sources aren't reporting it, America is now being run by a triad of huge conglomerates: JPMorganChase, Goldman Sachs and Bank of America. This is one of the reasons why the entire bailout took

ROB BLAGOJEVICH

JOHN SMIERCIAK/GETTY IMAGES

place—so that larger banks could swallow up smaller ones and centralize control. This power was evident on October 13, 2008 when Treasury Secretary Henry Paulson met with the capos of American banking to plan the largest bailout in history. Among those seated at the table was Bank of America CEO Kenneth Lewis, whose annual salary is $20 million, while his stock holdings top out at over $110 million.

The writing on the wall couldn't be any clearer. No pipsqueak governor was going to play hardball with Bank of America (or their hand-picked president) and get away with it. Plus, since Obama was already connected to so many other questionable characters, such as Tony Rezko, terrorist William Ayers and Rev. Wright, they couldn't afford to let Blagojevich further taint their Ponzi scheme by airing all of Chicago's dirty laundry. So, as the entire country watched, they put the governor's head on a chopping block and declared, in effect "This is what happens if you mess with us."

Beware: a New World Order financial mafia is alive and well in America. What happened to Gov. Blagojevich is a fitting example of how they operate, and how they'll eat one of their own when necessary.

BARACK OBAMA

Barack Obama's Planned Medical Socialism Puts Big Brother In Charge Of Your Health Care

Originally published: April 20, 2009

A re you ready to be euthanized? If you're an elderly American, especially one who doesn't walk in lockstep with the New World Order's plans to rid our planet of "useless eaters," you better prepare yourself for this possibility. Although most people aren't aware of it, Barack Obama's February 2009 stimulus bill contained the most draconian legislation this nation has ever seen. Hidden within this thousand-page document was health legislation that affects every individual in the United States.

Obama touted this plan's urgent necessity, but what he really gave us is the first step toward European neo-socialism mixed with closed-market British rationing. Add a touch of Orwellian Big Brother collectivism, and it all eventually leads to gulag-style totalitarianism. Developed by Bilderberg and CFR member Tom Daschle in his book *Critical: What We Can Do About the Health-Care Crisis*, we're now facing another big government takeover that has dire consequences if we ever get sick.

In simplest terms, a new bureaucracy will be formed, headed by a national coordinator of health information technology. Using a vast computer database that they'd like to have online by 2014, all medical treatments, in addition to other potential details (such as tax records, bank statements, police reports and "lifestyle choices") will be tracked electronically. According to Betsy McCaughey's seminal February 9 article, *Ruin Your Health with the Obama Stimulus Plan*, this board will "monitor treatments to make sure your doctor is doing what the federal government deems appropriate and cost effective."

Rather than abiding by the Hippocratic Oath where the safe treatment of each patient takes precedence, this new agency will only proceed with a procedure if there is a distinct payoff for society. This paradigm shift in perspective is where Daschle's worldview becomes horrifying. In his book, he praises Europeans who accept their "hopeless diagnoses." In contrast, he feels Americans still expect too much from the healthcare system and should instead simply "accept the conditions that come with age."

Writing for *Town Hall* on February 15, Austin Hill begins, "Welcome to the era of Obama. You now have a duty to die." Since doctors and hospitals will surrender their autonomy to a council of national coordinators who guide their decisions, Hill describes how "we now have the beginnings of a governmental agency that eventually will, by force of law, determine which persons will be eligible for healthcare, and what treatment they will receive."

If you're elderly, already sick with a preexisting condition, or have few years left to work, then according to Daschle and Obama's board, you have a "low return on investment," and as such, it's your duty to die. If you refuse to follow these edicts, then bureaucrats get to play God by deciding who should perish by denying medical treatment.

Hill makes it crystal clear. "Once you have lived 'long enough,' after you have consumed your 'fair share' of the Earth's resources; and when your combined age and health conditions make it 'obvious' that further efforts to prolong your life just simply 'aren't worth it,' you will then have a responsibility to accept these consequences, and to accept that you'll just have to get along without life-sustaining healthcare."

To ensure that these policies are followed, the bill refers to doctors becoming "meaningful users" who must become part of the system or face losing their license and/or government Medicare contracts. After studying this legislation, journalist Byron Richards discovered that the "quality and type of care will not be determined by the doctor, but rather by a new system of cost containment implemented by the federal government."

As an incentive, the board will give doctors bonuses (i.e. economic blackmail) if they comply with their mandates. Not only will they be encouraged to enter a patient's EHR (electronic health records), but they must also practice the "proper" kind of medicine. Wholistics, vitamin therapy, alternative procedures, plus new remedies or technologies that drive up costs

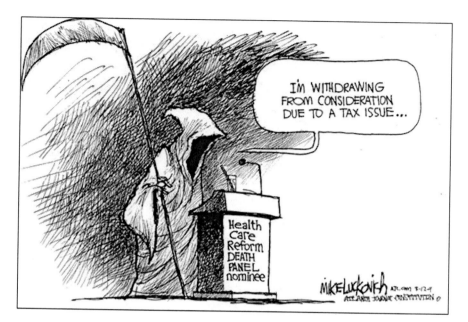

will be frowned upon. Under this plan, the board will issue life-and-death verdicts that politicians can safely stay distanced from. Or, as Tom Daschle recommends, senior citizens will have to accept conditions associated with old age because doctors will no longer be treating them.

To put the magnitude of this legislation into focus, Betsey McCaughey states that our country's largest employer is the health care industry, comprising 17 percent of GDP. Under Obama's plan, "The bill allocates more funding to this bureaucracy than for the Army, Navy, Marines and Air Force combined." Fearing a repeat of Hillary Clinton's healthcare debacle in 1994, Daschle urged the president to sneak this legislation into another bill before any opposition arises, therefore bypassing Congress.

Once the records of every American are entered into a labyrinthian electronic database, what comes next? Will our DNA samples soon be digitized, followed by computer microchips implanted into our bodies? We've just entered a *Brave New World* that is terrifying in its reach, intrusiveness and disregard for the sanctity of human life.

Inconsistencies Arise
In CFO Suicide Story

Originally published: May 11, 2009

Reminiscent of the ongoing microbiologist body count that AMERI-CAN FREE PRESS has reported on, a new wave of suicides is plaguing the financial industry, culminating in the recent death of Freddie Mac CFO David Kellermann.

The 41-year-old husband and father, described as having a life-of-the-party personality, was found dead in the basement of his $900,000 Vienna, Virginia home at 4:48 on the morning of April 22. Initially, "a law enforcement official speaking on condition of anonymity told the *Associated Press* that Kellermann hanged himself."

Other news agencies ran with this account, but then "Sabrina Rock, a Fairfax County police spokesman, confirmed to the AP that Kellermann was dead, but she could not confirm that he committed suicide despite WUSA reporting that Fairfax police told them it was suicide."

Stranger yet, police spokesman Lucy Caldwell told *All Headline News* editor Linda Young via telephone on April 22 that "other people were present at the home at the time of Kellermann's death, "and that" there was a gun and a gunshot wound."

If true, this final variable is explosive for one obvious reason. How often does a suicide victim hang himself, then shoot himself; or shoot himself first, then hang himself? Considering these conflicting accounts, conspiracy theorists almost immediately began speculating. Some compared this scenario to the murder of Vince Foster; while others claimed Kellermann became a fall guy for Sen. Christopher Dodd (D-Conn.) and Rep. Barney Frank (D-Mass.), or the architects behind Barack Obama's economic plan.

COMPANY MAN

To determine whether this conjecture is valid, we need to first examine Mr. Kellermann's role at Freddie Mac. Employed at this government-sponsored mortgage firm since 1992, Kellermann served as a financial analyst, principal accounting officer, corporate controller and senior vice president, and was then finally promoted to CFO in September 2008. Loyal, driven and working strenuously long hours, he typified the ultimate "company man."

Unfortunately, Freddie Mac came to be recognized as a primary catalyst for the ill-fated housing bubble's collapse where perilously risky loans led to record-setting defaults. Matthew Barakat and Alan Zibel of the Associated Press noted on April 23 that "the company lost $50 billion last year, and the Treasury Department has pumped in $45 billion to keep the company afloat." To make matters worse, Freddie Mac was the subject of federal investigations by the Securities and Exchange Commission, as well as the Justice Department. The focus of their probes revolved around the accounting practices used for their 13 million mortgages. With serious doubts surfacing about the validity of Obama's Troubled Assets Relief Program (TARP), Freddie Mac and Fannie Mae have come under increased scrutiny, especially since, as Christine Seib of the *Times UK* wrote on April 22, they "lend or guarantee half of America's $12 trillion mortgage market."

The stress at Freddie Mac became so pronounced that Barakat and Zibel reported, "Last month, David Moffett, the government-appointed chief executive, resigned in frustration over strict oversight." To complicate matters, the public's fury over executive bonuses directly affected Kellermann. CNBC on-air editor Charlie Gasparino summarized the situation on April 22. "In March, Kellermann was one of a handful of senior Freddie Mac people to have received a bonus, in his case $850,000, which prompted criticism and outrage." The blowback alarmed Kellermann, as *Clusterstock* editor Joe Weisenthal documents. "Reporters and camera crews showed up at his home in an affluent Washington suburb. Fearing that someone might attack his house, his wife or their five-year-old daughter, he asked the company to provide a security detail."

COOKING THE BOOKS

The question remains: what was Kellermann's role in Freddie Mac's meltdown? Being a key insider with access to highly sensitive material, did he help facilitate the accounting gimmicks that brought about his company's demise? Or, could Kellermann have been one of the good guys who refused to perpetuate this ruse being foisted on American taxpayers? To his credit, Barakat and Zibel indicate, "Kellermann was neither a target nor a subject of the [U.S. attorney's] investigation, and had not been under law enforcement scrutiny."

Freddie Mac had been subpoenaed, however, for documents relating to its accounting and disclosure improprieties. Was the entire house of cards beginning to crumble, and instead of covering it up, Kellermann instead intended to come clean? What makes this matter suspicious is that only one day prior to his death, the Associated Press reported on April 21 that "a human resources officer met with Kellermann and told him he needed a break because he had been working so hard." Faced with a much-needed vacation to spend time with his wife and daughter, why would Kellermann suddenly choose to kill himself? Or was Freddie Mac clandestinely trying to push its top executive out the door in a roundabout way?

SMOKE & MIRRORS

The most pressing issue on the table at this time was Freddie Mac's first-quarter financial reports, which Kellermann proposed to release at the end of May. Matters became extremely complicated because "Freddie Mac executives recently battled with federal regulators over whether to disclose potential losses on mortgage securities tied to the Obama administration's housing plan" (Zibel and Barakat, April 22).

The crux of this subject is now apparent. A massive battle ensued between federal regulators who were trying to cover up catastrophic economic news, and those who refused to further cook the books. Zachary Goldfarb and Jonathan Mummolo of *The Washington Post* provided invaluable insight on April 23. "Kellermann figured in several recent controversies at Freddie Mac. He and a group of company attorneys tussled with regulators in early March as the firm prepared to file its quarterly earnings report with the Securities and Exchange Commission. The group insisted that Freddie Mac inform shareholders of the cost to the company in helping carry out the Obama administration's housing recovery plan. The regulators urged the company not to do so."

An industry veteran who wished to remain anonymous offered the following assessment for *Housing Wire*. "This isn't the story of a guy who was trying to cover something up. It's the story of a guy who was trying to do the right thing. Kellermann and his cohorts insisted on reporting Freddie Mac's financial status as they believed it should be reported, disclosing all of its obligations."

Did Kellermann's smoking gun information (and that held by other top executive who've been "suicided" in recent months) ultimately cost him his life?

Obama White House
To Waffling Law Firm:
'Chrysler Deal an Offer
You Just Can't Refuse'

Originally published: May 25, 2009

Are fascist thug tactics now becoming the part-and-parcel norm for Barack Obama and his henchmen? In previous chapters, I detailed serious allegations concerning the mysterious deaths of a 47-year-old choirmaster and two other young black men who attended Obama's Trinity United Church of Christ (whose former pastor was Rev. Jeremiah Wright). More recently, Freddie Mac CFO David Kellermann was found "suicided" in his basement prior to releasing some very damning financial information regarding the housing market.

Now, during the first week of May, attorney Thomas Lauria disclosed in an interview on Detroit's WJR-AM radio that Perella Weinberg Partners was being strong-armed by Obama officials in regard to the Chrysler bankruptcy offer. On May 2, he told host Frank Beckmann, "One of my clients was directly threatened by the White House and, in essence, compelled to withdraw its opposition to the [bankruptcy] deal under the threat that the full force of the White House press corps would destroy its reputation if it continued to fight."

The individual spearheading this clandestine campaign was Steve Rattner, head of Obama's Auto Industry Task Force. Rattner, it must be noted, was an important Democratic Party fundraiser during the 2008 campaign, and is now embroiled in a pay-to-play kickback scandal. He also has no experience whatsoever in the auto industry. Almost immediately, White

House officials denied that any such juggernaut existed in which investors were pressured into accepting their deal. Then, dramatically, on May 3, a post on *The New York Times* Deal Book blog reported that Perella Weinberg accepted the "government-proposed settlement after Mr. Obama criticized the lenders in harsh terms." They also proceeded to "deny Mr. Lauria's account of events."

Despite conflicting stories, the question remains: Did White House representatives—and the president himself—utilize a well-calculated campaign of fear by threatening to ruin or destroy the reputation of certain companies if they didn't fall in line? Before providing an answer, let's hark back to an incident that occurred in October 2008 when Treasury Secretary Henry Paulson gathered executives from America's nine largest banks in a room, then gave each a one-page document and said, "No one is leaving this room until it's signed." Reluctantly, all nine agreed, setting in motion what investment advisor Michael Shedlock called "the largest government intervention in the American banking system since the Depression."

Working hand in hand with Paulson at that time was the current treasury secretary, Timothy Geithner, who helped mastermind the disastrous bailout scheme that is wreaking so much havoc on our economy. Part of this package involved the bailout, and subsequent bankruptcy, of Chrysler Motors. Under the Obama-Geithner settlement deal, bondholders were to receive approximately 29 cents on the dollar owed them. Not satisfied with this arrangement, especially when the United Auto Workers (UAW) received a much sweeter deal, Perella Weinberg (through its subsidiary Xerion Fund) balked at the offer.

Now remember, White House officials said that no undue pressure was exerted, nor did they attempt to ruin anyone's reputation. But on April 31—the deadline date for Chrysler's overhaul—President Obama directly targeted Perella Weinberg and threw them under the bus.

"While many stakeholders made sacrifices and worked constructively, I have to tell you, some did not. In particular, a group of investment firms and hedge funds decided to hold out for the prospect of an unjustified taxpayer-funded bailout. They were hoping that everybody else would make sacrifices, and they would have to make none." He then concluded by saying, "I don't stand with them."

For starters, how could the loss of 70 cents on every dollar not be con-

Officials listen intently at hearings held to determine the fate of Chrysler Corp.

sidered a sacrifice? Secondly, as attorney Tom Lauria professed, "It's no fun standing on this side of the fence opposing the president of the United States." He continued, "He stands my clients up as basically the reason Chrysler is going into bankruptcy. He wrongly says they're not willing to make any sacrifices. People are scared. They have gotten death threats. Some have been told people are going to come to their houses."

On the heels of David Kellermann's unfortunate "demise," ABC's Jake Tapper wrote on May 2 that Perella Weinberg (via Xerion Fund), "decided to join the larger four creditors who are owed roughly 70% of Chrysler's debt and had already agreed to participate with the administration's plan."

Incidentally, the other four creditors referred to are—JP Morgan Chase, Citigroup, Morgan Stanley and Goldman Sachs—all recipients of billions in bailout money orchestrated by Timothy Geithner and company. Of course, as Tapper asserts somewhat sarcastically, "The Obama administration insists these matters were kept completely separate." Isn't it funny how things work out that way? Benito Mussolini's OVRA, or secret police, would be extremely pleased with these tactics.

JOE BIDEN AND BARACK OBAMA

Biden Blasted For 'Bunker' Blunder; Cheney's 9-11 Actions Re-Examined

Originally published: June 8, 2009

Once again, mainstream media sources failed to report the real story behind the story. On May 17, Eleanor Clift, *Newsweek's* contributing editor, dished up another tasty entrée of Joe Biden's specialty—foot-in-the-mouth *du jour*. At the Gridiron Club's annual white-tie gala, the vice president disclosed classified information regarding Dick Cheney's infamous underground bunker beneath the Naval Observatory in D.C.

Being that Biden took over residence from Cheney in the vice presidential manor this past January, he related to fellow diners (journalists included) how a young naval tour guide "showed him the hideaway, which is behind a massive steel door secured by an elaborate lock with a narrow connecting hallway lined with shelves filled with communications equipment." Clift continued, "The officer explained that when Cheney was in lockdown, this was where his most trusted aides were stationed."

Heckled by pundits for the umpteenth time, Biden dismissed his statements by saying that he was actually referring to an "upstairs workspace." But his words were obviously misleading because in December 2002, neighbors living adjacent to the vice president's residence complained of "strange explosions" emanating from beneath Cheney's home. In response, the Naval Observatory's superintendent sent each a letter. "Due to its sensitive nature in support of national security and homeland defense, this project's specific information is classified and cannot be released." This memo also stressed, "The work was urgent and needed to be done on a highly accelerated schedule." In a *Dr. Strangelove*-style twist, Cheney (who denied the very existence of this "Bat Cave") ordered Google to obscure his residence from their satellite maps (which they did).

CHENEY AND 9-11

With these revelations in mind, some commentators have erroneously stated that vice president Cheney hunkered down in this bunker during the 9-11 "terrorist attacks." But as I stated, construction didn't officially begin on this enclave until December 2002. In actuality, at approximately 9:10 to 9:20 a.m. on September 11, Cheney scurried to the Presidential Emergency Operations Center (PEOC) beneath the White House East Wing. Here, a crucial event took place that had a profound effect on the purported Pentagon strike.

According to Transportation Secretary Norman Mineta, he entered the PEOC at 9:25 or 9:26 a.m., whereupon he witnessed an aide repeatedly giving the vice president frantic updates. He provided the following public testimony to the 9-11 Commission on April 23, 2003.

> During the time that the airplane [Flight 77] was coming in to the Pentagon, there was a young man who would come in to say to the vice president, "The plane is 50 miles out." "The plane is 30 miles out." And when it got down to "the plane is 10 miles out," the young man also said to the vice president, "Do the orders still stand?" The vice president turned and whipped his neck around and said, "Of course the orders still stand. Have you heard anything to the contrary?"

Now, as most prudent observers realize, Flight 77 never struck the Pentagon. But, an event did take place at 9:38 a.m. where a certain amount of damage occurred, resulting in 125 deaths. But what are we to make of the "orders" that this aide questioned Dick Cheney about? In an excellent article by Professor David Ray Griffin on April 28, 2008 entitled *9-11 Contradictions: When Did Cheney Enter the Underground Bunker*, he writes, "The expected orders, especially on a day when two hijacked airliners had already crashed into buildings in New York, would have been to shoot down any non-military aircraft entering the 'prohibited' airspace over Washington."

But since Cheney was repeatedly asked about these "orders," Griffin concludes quite perceptively: "The question made sense only if the orders were to do something unusual—not to shoot the aircraft down. It appeared, accordingly, that Mineta had inadvertently reported Cheney's confirmation of stand-down orders."

Obviously, Flight 77 was never shot down over our nation's capital (nor did it strike the Pentagon). In a May 5, 2008 article, 9-11 researcher Aidan Monaghan stresses that ample notice was given to government officials. "The FAA notified the military about the suspected hijacking of Flight 77 at 9:24 a.m., if not before. The FBI's Washington field office was also notified that Flight 77 had been hijacked at about 9:20 a.m." In essence, the Pentagon and White House had an eternity to react, but failed to do so. Somebody ordered the stand-down and, operationally at least, one of those men was Dick Cheney.

THE ARMAGEDDON PLAN

Cheney and Defense Secretary Donald Rumsfeld's hands-on involvement in the execution of 9-11 can be traced back to what journalist James Mann calls "The Armageddon Plan" in the March 2004 issue of *The Atlantic* magazine. During the Reagan administration—when Cold War paranoia still ran high—Cheney and Rumsfeld joined 40 to 60 other federal officials in a highly classified program dealing with COG (continuity of government).

During these secretive operations, various shadow government teams were formed in the event of a nuclear strike by the Soviets. In an article for *The Guardian* by Tom Vanderbilt entitled "Is This Bush's Secret Bunker?", he describes how "the president could repair to Mount Weather; Congress had its secret bunker in Culpeper, Virginia; the Pentagon was given a rocky redoubt called Site R [Raven Rock] in the mountains of southwest Pennsylvania; while the nation's air defenses were run out of NORAD." Vanderbilt describes Mount Weather as "a sprawling underground complex bristling with mainframe computers, air circulation pumps, and a television/radio studio for post-nuclear presidential broadcasts."

As each of these teams was dispatched to clandestine locales, mock "presidents" were appointed to each. Not surprisingly, both Cheney and Rumsfeld were designated to be "commanders-in-chief" of their respective squadrons. Mann also explains how "the capstone to all these efforts was a special airplane, the National Emergency Airborne Command Post, a modified Boeing 747 based at Andrews Air Force Base and specially outfitted with a conference room and advanced communications gear. In it, a president could remain in the air and run the country during a nuclear showdown."

Considering these words, let's fast-forward to September 11, 2001 when bedlam broke loose in D.C. As Mann concludes in his expose, "Cheney and Rumsfeld suddenly began to act out parts of a script they had rehearsed years before. Operating from the underground shelter beneath the White House, called the Presidential Emergency Operations Center, Cheney told Bush to delay a planned flight back from Florida to Washington." In the meantime, Rumsfeld sent others, like Paul Wolfowitz, to out-of-town bunkers.

In essence, while one team of conspirators ran the show in New York City from Rudy Giuliani's Office of Emergency Management on the 23rd floor of WTC 7, another team consisting of Cheney, Rumsfeld and Gen. Richard Meyers hearkened back to their special training via the Armageddon Plan. When questioned a few days after 9-11 by NBC's Tim Russert in regard to their actions at the time, Cheney responded furtively, "We did a lot of planning during the Cold War with respect to the possibility of a nuclear incident."

When Joe Biden spilled the beans about Cheney's not-so-secret bunker, he didn't know how closely he came to opening up an entirely different can of worms.

Hillary, Bill & Barack's ACORN Connection

Originally published: June 22, 2009

Similar to Dick Cheney's Halliburton, Richard Nixon's Watergate and the Clintons' Whitewater scandal, ACORN is becoming a public relations albatross around Barack Obama's neck. With the Feds investigating ACORN in a dozen states (voter fraud, accounting irregularities etc.) and confirmation that the founder's brother—Dale Rathke—embezzled nearly a million dollars, a critical eye is now being cast by reporters, political pundits and possibly Congress.

By their own admission, ACORN covered up Rathke's illegal activities to keep law enforcement off its heels; while in May, *The New York Times* confessed to spiking a pre-election story that connected ACORN to Barack Obama. This article has been described as "game changing" and could have swayed the 2008 presidential outcome.

As more researchers pry into the shady dealings of ACORN, Service Employee International Union (SEIU), and the privately owned Citizens Consulting, Inc. (CCI); an interesting sidebar has emerged. In 1970, Wade Rathke set up shop in Little Rock, Arkansas—home of the notorious Dixie Mafia and one of the most corrupt venues imaginable. A long-time Rockefeller stronghold operated by kingmakers Witt and Jackson Stephens, this region also came under the heavy thumb of Sen. J. William Fulbright (a globalist Rhodes scholar), Don Tyson, Dan Lasater, the Clinton-created ADFA, BCCI and some extremely criminal activity at an airstrip in Mena.

Richard Odom summarizes the commingling of high finance and the underworld in his fine book *Circle of Death*. "If Arkansas of the 1980s was something of a regional center for banking and small industry, it was also an international center for drug smuggling, gun-running and money laundering operations."

Since Arkansas is at the nexus of this brewing firestorm, naturally Bill and Hillary Clinton gravitated toward the cesspool. The website *Founding Bloggers* states, "The connections between Wade Rathke (founder of ACORN) and the Clintons go way back. Don't forget, the "A" in ACORN originally stood for Arkansas [i.e. Arkansas Community Organization for Reform Now]."

While initially conceived as an offshoot of radical socialist George Wiley's National Welfare Reform Organization (NWRO), ACORN quickly became more political by running and endorsing candidates in local elections. One of the first politicians they backed was a rising 32-year-old star named Bill Clinton, who became the youngest governor in the nation at the time. In a seminal book on Arkansas' favorite son entitled *On the Make*, journalist Meredith Oakley notes that "ACORN gave early publicity and fund-raising to Clinton due to his anti-utilities stance."

Needless to say, ACORN became intertwined with another charismatic young politician—Chicago's Barack Obama—who worked on one of their voter registration projects after receiving his law degree from Harvard. Although separated by time and locale, the links between these figures is uncanny (and most certainly not coincidental).

For starters, Hillary Clinton wrote her senior honors thesis at Wellesley College on Chicago's radical left-wing activist, Saul Alinsky. After forming ACORN in Little Rock, Wade Rathke enrolled his new recruits into a program at Syracuse University that was based on Alinsky's teachings. Rathke began his career as a "draft-resistance organizer for the Students for a Democratic Society (SDS)," whereas Bill Clinton used every conceivable power broker in Arkansas to facilitate his draft-dodging efforts.

Another famous SDS alumnus was William Ayers, himself a Saul Alinsky protégé and future Weather Underground terrorist. Of course, Barack Obama kicked-off his political career with a fundraiser at Ayers's home, while also working with him on the Woods Fund and Annenberg Challenge. Similarly, when the Clintons rendered their famous pardon-gate before leaving the White House in 2001, they included two key members of the Weather Underground.

While establishing itself in the early 1970s, ACORN's state chairwoman

Dorothy Perkins labeled them "one of the biggest scams in Arkansas." An October 13, 2008 article on the website *Founding Bloggers* clearly shows how this corruption led straight to the governor's mansion. "ACORN was an off-shoot of the SDS/Weather Underground, and they had done a lot of crooked stuff under (and for) Clinton back in Arkansas, and then in the general elections. They knew where Clinton's skeletons were buried, and so, he took care of them."

Bill and Hillary learned their lessons well, for in the 1980s they established the Arkansas Development Finance Authority (ADFA) that took campaign financing to all-time lows. In essence, reminiscent of tactics used by BCCI, money laundered from Iran-Contra drugs-and-arms sales was funneled into the ADFA, which was supposedly started to assist low-income home buyers, small businesses, and to create jobs. But, akin to ACORN, a far different picture emerged. According to David Bresnahan in *Damage Control*, "In seven years, ADFA created 2,751 jobs. Each cost the taxpayer $13,202 to create—although the average salary was only $15,000."

There were other kickback scams, slush funds and, more importantly, millions of dollars directed into Bill Clinton's gubernatorial campaign coffers [not to mention his 1992 run for the Oval Office]. UK columnist Ambrose Evans-Pritchard called these funds "Bill Clinton's own political piggy bank." Also, it's now known that the ADFA worked hand-in-hand with Freddie Mac, Fannie Mae and ACORN to secure home loans (many of which turned out badly) for Arkansas residents who couldn't afford them. This practice soon spread nationwide, creating a housing bubble that led to our current economic despair.

The biggest variable right now is: why did black nationalist leader George Wiley (a predecessor to Barack Obama's spiritual advisor, Rev. Jeremiah Wright) send Wade Rathke to Little Rock, Arkansas? It's my contention that since Bill Clinton had long been selected to be the "chosen one," establishing ACORN in Arkansas was step one in mobilizing the SDS-Weather Underground-black nationalist-extreme socialist contingent to amass power in this country.

Their subversive efforts, although largely unnoticed for many years, were horrifyingly effective when viewed in the following context. If the same man owned the New York Yankees and New York Mets and both teams played in the World Series, would it matter to him which one won? No, because both are under his umbrella. Well, the 1992 election pitted progressive globalist George Bush Sr. against progressive globalist Bill Clinton. Slick Willie served for eight years, and became, by his own account, "America's first black president." Then, after George W. Bush's disastrous reign (where one Skull & Bonesman ran against another Skull & Bonesman [John Kerry] in 2004), it was an almost foregone conclusion that a Democrat would win in 2008.

As a result, in the primaries, Little Rock-transplant Hillary Clinton and Chicago's Barack Obama were both unabashed products of the above-mentioned political cabal. Obama got the nod, thus becoming America's second black ACORN-affiliated president.

America's Future Getting Darker: It Was the Black Harvard Professor, Not White Cop, Who Acted 'Stupidly'

Originally published: August 17, 2009

"Yeah, I'll speak with your mama outside." These are the words that Henry Louis Gates, a supposedly esteemed Harvard professor, sneered at James Crowley when the officer reported to a possible burglary at his residence on July 16. In reality, it's simply another example of how the entirety of our society is being degraded by a president who vowed during his campaign to "fundamentally transform the United States of America." Now we see black academicians obnoxiously popping off to policemen, using ghetto slang like they do in the 'hood. What makes matters even more appalling is that Barack Obama supported this race-baiting "intellectual" elitist during a nationally televised press conference on July 22. While directly admitting to "not having been there and seeing all the facts," Obama still proceeded to denigrate the Cambridge police department by saying they "acted stupidly."

POLITICAL THEATER

Before analyzing a few other pertinent details of this case, it must be made perfectly clear that this hot-button "news" item was nothing more than a deliberate set-up to distract attention from the fact that Obama's socialized healthcare scheme came crashing and burning down around him (at least temporarily). He then added to the mix a good old-fashioned dose of none-too-subtle racism (i.e. divide-and-conquer). The president had to rely on these tactics because Americans, congressmen and even many Democrats don't want to be saddled with trillions more in debt.

So, how could Obama—an attorney and very slick politician who's usually so in control—make such a huge, radioactive blunder? Well, he didn't. Rather, Obama simply followed a convenient script for Political Theater 101. Let's look at the players. First, the woman who asked the question at his press conference (which seemingly came from left field), was Lynn Sweet, a longtime media hack for the *Chicago Sun-Times*. Of course, Obama's hometown is Chicago, and Sweet has been a part of that corrupt crime machine for decades. Her con job became so evident that Sweet had to dismiss claims that any type of "conspiracy" existed or that she served as a "plant" for the administration.

The second figure in this charade is Professor Gates, who befriended the president many years earlier when Obama attended Harvard Law School. As such, Obama was well acquainted with each of these "inside" participants. The result is a rather obvious (and pathetic) attempt to shift attention away from their failures by pitting one element of society against another. It's the oldest trick in the book, and those who cry "police misconduct" are among the naïve and gullible who've fallen into a trap set by Rahm Emanuel and company.

REVERSE RACISM

This whole debacle started when Cambridge resident Lucia Whalen notified officials that "two large men" were forcibly trying to enter a home. [She never used the word "black" in describing them, thus eliminating any racial motive.] When Officer Crowley arrived on the scene and asked Gates (the possible suspect) for his I.D., the professor erupted, "Why? Because I'm a black man in America?" While Crowley remained calm and businesslike, Gates initially refused to show his license. Then he threatened, "You have no idea who you're messing with" and "you haven't heard the last of me."

Gates' belligerent, irrational and uncooperative behavior is even more puzzling when considering his home was broken into a few months earlier; that's why the lock remained jammed. Instead of being grateful for his concern, Gates continued to yell and call Crowley a "racist cop." Drawing a crowd and other police officers, he was eventually arrested for disorderly conduct after being given several warnings. Ms. Whalen later verified that Gates alone escalated the situation.

But, according to Gates, ulterior motives came into play. He reportedly told an interviewer, "He's just angry because he's a poor white cop, and I'm a rich black intellectual, and he's trying to level the playing field."

This type of perpetual victimization espoused by those with slave-reparation mentalities was reflected in the comments of Opio Sokoni, the black founder of Poli-tainment, Inc. During a July 24 appearance on *Fox News* with Mike Huckabee, he equated today's policemen with being "descendants of the Ku Klux Klan."

When President Obama chose to insinuate himself into this local law enforcement issue, it not only made him look petty and foolish, it also reflected his own deeply ingrained racism. On July 24, black Rev. Jesse Lee Peterson (president and founder of BOND) minced no words. "Barack Obama was wrong to malign and insult the Cambridge police department. [His] words were racist and irresponsible. He owes the nation an apology." Peterson added during a televised interview on July 24 that, "Obama hates the white man." He also released a written statement on this same date stating that the president's stance "validates black hatred of whites and police officers."

TRUE COLORS

When asked whether he'd apologize, Officer Crowley responded firmly, "No." And he shouldn't. Not only was he simply doing his job, a black police sergeant actually chose him to head the department's sensitivity training program.

One wonders why President Obama so carelessly thrust himself into this fracas. One clue may be that he used to live in this very community while attending the Harvard Law School. There, he received a slew of parking tickets that went unpaid for decades, possibly leading to long-term resentment against the police force. The Associated Press reported on March 8, 2007, "The Illinois senator shelled out $375 in January—two weeks before he officially launched his presidential campaign—to finally pay for fifteen outstanding parking tickets and their associated late fees." How convenient, reminiscent of Treasury Secretary Timothy Geithner "forgetting" to pay his income taxes until he was up for nomination.

Akin to his twenty-year relationship with the racist, black nationalist preacher, Rev. Jeremiah Wright, as each day passes, Barack Obama continues to show his true colors. As a result of his actions and prejudiced perspective, America's future keeps getting darker and darker.

GEORGE SOROS

Who Is Behind Obama's Rise to Political Stardom

Originally published: August 17, 2009

Is Barack Obama the product of a vast socialist conspiracy designed to undermine the fundamental tenets established by our Founding Fathers, all bankrolled and organized by Jewish financiers? The answer is unequivocally: yes.

To deconstruct this labyrinth-like network, one must start at the top with businessman George Soros and his ties to the world's most powerful Zionist family. Journalist, historian and economic researcher William Engdahl sets the stage. "Soros has been identified as a front man for the Rothschild banking group. Understandably, neither he nor the Rothschilds want this important fact to be public." He continues, "Soros's connections to the ultra-secret international finance circles of the Rothschilds is not just an ordinary or accidental banking connection." Finally, in a November 1, 1996 article, Engdahl writes, "From the very first days when Soros created his own investment fund in 1969, he owed his success to his relation to the Rothschild family banking network."

Soros, through his Open Society Institute, funnels approximately $300 million a year into various liberal venues, including the influential MoveOn.org. According to veteran researcher Anton Chaitkin, Soros also hand picked Barack Obama to challenge Hillary Clinton (and ultimately defeat GOP nominee John McCain). On September 5, 2008, he wrote, "Barack Obama came under special Soros sponsorship in the 2004 U.S. Senate race [and] raised $60,000 for his campaign." After attaining victory, Obama met personally with Soros, then attended a fundraiser at his home.

Chaitkin elaborates further in *Soros Runs British Foreign Office Coup*

Against U.S. Elections: "On December 4, 2006, two years after getting into the U.S. Senate, Barack Obama went to Soros's New York office to be interviewed for higher office. Soros then took Obama into a conference room for other politically subordinate billionaires. With money and connections ensured, Obama announced for the presidency soon afterward."

ANATOMY OF A CONSPIRACY

To understand how devastating this Rothschild-Soros agenda is, we need to look at the words of Michelle Obama in a June 19, 2008 speech where she said, "We're going to have to change our traditions and our history." In other words, Obama & Company is trying to alter the very fabric upon which this country was founded. She explained further on August 25, 2008: "All of us are driven by a simple belief that the world as it is just won't do. We have an obligation to fight for the world as it should be."

Who, precisely, will determine how our world should be? Mrs. Obama's poignant phrase was lifted directly from Saul Alinsky, a Chicago-based Jewish extremist who penned the handbook for far-left causes, *Rules for Radicals*. To implement his plans to undermine America, an intricate network needed to be established that would spread its tentacles throughout every aspect of society.

One of the primary vehicles they utilized was the Tides Foundation, to which Soros contributed $13 million from 1997 to 2003. Established by Jewish antiwar activist Drummond Pike in 1976, this tax-exempt organization serves a very important function. According to researcher Ben Johnson of *Front Page Magazine* in September 2004, they "allow high-profile individuals to fund extremist organizations by 'laundering' their money through Tides, leaving no paper trail."

In essence, after taking a ten-percent cut, Tides has fed over $300 million to entities such as cop killer Mumia Abu-Jamal, MoveOn.org and those who advocate abortion-on-demand, all the while assuring contributors that they won't be publicly linked to these causes. One look at the Tides Foundations' board reveals who calls the shots. Drummond, Senior Vice President Gary Schwartz, and Executive Vice President Ellen Friedman are all Jewish.

Pike also used his leverage to bail out ACORN's welfare rights leader Wade Rathke after he embezzled $948,507. To protect Rathke, ACORN never contacted law enforcement officials or sought prosecution. Instead, Stephanie Strom of *The New York Times* wrote on August 17, 2008, "The organization announced that an anonymous supporter had agreed" to pay off the debt. That man was Drummond Pike. To cover the group's tracks, Arthur Schwartz (Jewish) now coordinates its slippery public relations.

Of course, Barack Obama began his political career as the chief national trainer for ACORN, which now faces lawsuits in fourteen states for voter fraud. Obama's mentor as a community organizer in Chicago was Gerald Kellman (Jewish), a Saul Alinksy protégé. To begin his meteoric rise toward the White House, money originated from what Clarice Feldman of *American Thinker* calls the "Gang of Four"—Soros, Peter Lewis, Stephen Bing and Herbert and Marion Sandler. All are Jewish billionaires.

One of Obama's most important backers was Marilyn Katz (Jewish), who oversaw security for the SDS (Students for a Democratic Society) and advocated violent guerrilla tactics toward the police (as did Obama associate William Ayers of the Weather Underground). Katz became a fundraising bundler for Obama, as well as hosting fundraisers and serving as an Illinois delegate at the 2008 Democratic National Convention.

GREEN MOVEMENT AND HEALTHCARE

The Tides Foundation controls the San Francisco-based Apollo Alliance, which "absolutely believes that government is the solution to all social and economic problems." On July 28, Phil Kerpen of *Americans for Prosperity* described how the "Apollo Alliance is designed to bring together the elements of organized labor with community organizers and green groups." More importantly, Kerpen revealed that the Apollo Alliance "put out a draft stimulus bill in 2008 … that included almost everything that ended up being in the final stimulus bill."

Van Jones, Obama's new "green jobs czar," described the Apollo Alliance as a "grand unified field theory for progressive left causes." Who exactly is Van Jones? After participating in the 1992 L.A. riots (for which he was arrested and incarcerated), Jones told the *East Bay Express* on November 2, 2005, "I met all these young radical people of color—I mean, really radical communists and anarchists. And it was like: this is what I need to be part of. I spent the next ten years of my life working with a lot of these people I met in jail, trying to be a revolutionary. I was a rowdy black revolutionary on April 28, and when the verdicts came down on April 29, I was a communist."

To round out this list, the Service Employees International Union (SEIU) is primarily responsible for what is contained in Obama's socialized healthcare bill. Andy Stern and Anna Burger lead the SEIU, both of whom are Jewish cronies of George Soros. Their vice president is Gerald Hudson (Jewish). Pushing this bill and the stimulus package to various media outlets is Robert Borosage (Jewish) of the Institute for America's Future (also a huge recipient of Soros' funding). Overseeing the housing and banking industries is none other than Barney Frank (Jewish), chairman of the House Financial Services Committee. Last but not least, most of Obama's inner circle—David Axelrod, Lawrence Summers, Rahm Emanuel, Paul Volcker and Timothy Geithner—are Jewish (although some sources say Geithner is not).

TRUTH EXPOSED

Putting this complicated matter into perspective is educational theorist and critic David Solway. On July 7, 2009 he wrote, "We Jews are a sly and surreptitious people. It pains me to admit this, but candor compels. We have understood that the best way to bring America to its knees, to weaken its will to survive, to cleverly turn it against itself, was to do everything in our considerable arsenal of means to deliver the White House to Barack Obama."

The conspiracy has been completed, and now the Jewish Rothschild-Soros connection controls voter registration (ACORN), money laundering (Tides), billions in stimulus spending (Apollo), possibly the future of healthcare (SEIU), finance (Franks) and the Oval Office's inner workings (Emanuel, Geithner, Axelrod and Summers). Ironically, after Obama was forced to separate himself from spiritual adviser Jeremiah Wright, the reverend complained, "Them Jews aren't going to let him talk to me."

Obama's Cabinet of Death: Some Say 'Obamacare' No More Than Slow-Motion Euthanasia

Originally published: August 31, 2009

Deep in the corridors of President Obama's White House lurk death-mongers with little to no regard for human life. These czars and appointed officials follow the lead of their commander-in-chief, who was one of only five senators to vote in opposition to a ban on the gruesome practice of partial-birth abortion (October 2007). As an Illinois state senator, Obama inconceivably voted twice against the Induced Infant Liability Act, which gave protection to babies born of botched abortions. In other words, if an aborted baby survived, it would simply be placed in an incubator until starvation set in because the mother intended it to die. When registered nurse Jill Stanek showed photographs of these fully alive children to Obama—babies that would be permitted to die—she said, "Those pictures didn't faze him at all." His cold-bloodedness also became evident during the 2008 presidential campaign when declaring that his biggest congressional mistake was a vote in favor of saving Terri Schiavo's life.

DEATH PANELS

As senior citizens caught a glimpse of Obama's proposed "death panels," they reacted with outrage this summer at town hall meetings. Although his handlers tried to misdirect attention, Obama himself confirmed their existence. When David Leonhardt of *The New York Times* asked on April 28 how he'd deal with those "toward the end of their lives," his response was: "You have to have some independent group that can give you guidance."

Specifically, Section 1233 of the House bill would appoint death counselors on "the use of artificially administered nutrition and hydration and other end of life treatments."

Blowback was swift and immediate. Former New York Lieutenant Governor Betsy McCaughey remarked, "This consultation is essentially an attempt to kill off elderly Americans." Andy Martin's (R-Ill.) July 23 comments were even more direct. "What Barack Obama wants to do is slowly withdraw healthcare from our elderly population. He wants to target the most vulnerable in our society for extermination through bureaucratic empowerment. Obamacare is nothing more than slow-motion euthanasia in the guise of cost control."

Similarly, RA analyst Marie Jon cut through the rhetoric. "Advance Care Planning is code words for a mandated medical death sentence." In an article for the *American Thinker* on July 26, John Griffing hit a New World Order nerve. "Today's Medicare recipients could be the first to experience our government's new solution to America's 'useless eaters.'" Finally, as an alternative, representative Virginia Foxx (R-N.C.) told her colleagues on the House floor (July 28) that they needed a plan that "will not put seniors in a position of being put to death by their government."

SCIENCE CZAR

Possibly the most diabolical individual in Obama's Cabinet is Science Czar John Holdren, whose extremist views were exposed in his book *Eco-science*. Below is a sampling of what he proposed (all verbatim quotations):

- Compulsory population-control laws, even laws requiring compulsory abortion, could be sustained under the existing Constitution.
- The development of a long-term sterilizing capsule that could be implanted under the skin and removed when pregnancy is desired opens additional possibilities for coercive fertility control.
- Adding a sterilant to drinking water or staple foods is a suggestion that seems to horrify people more than most proposals for involuntary fertility control.

Holdren also intimates that newborn babies aren't yet "fully human," and that a transnational "planetary regime" should be enacted to, as Matt Barber of *Life News* wrote on July 23, "enforce mandatory abortions for population control and limit the use of natural resources."

DOCTOR DEATH AND THE BABY KILLER

As Kansas Governor, Health and Human Services Secretary Kathleen Sebelius was notable in her ardent support (and cover-up) of the practices of slain abortion doctor, George Tiller "the Baby Killer." Even after patients recounted horror stories of his butcher-like practices, Tiller still contributed over $30,000 to various of Sebelius's campaigns, and was only one of three doctors who practiced partial-birth abortion in America (even nine months into a woman's pregnancy). Further, Sebelius was nominated for her current position after Obama's original selection, former Sen. Tom Daschle, resigned under a cloud of controversy due to income tax invasion. Daschle gained notoriety for his advocacy of European-style universal healthcare where seniors are (according to harsh critics) expected to fulfill their "duty to die" for the betterment of society.

On the other hand, Obama's health care czar is the brother of Israeli dual-citizen, Rahm Emanuel. Known as "Doctor Death," Ezekiel Emanuel has authored such articles as:

- "What Are the Potential Cost Savings from Legalizing Physician-Assisted Suicide?"
- "Choosing the Time to Die: The Ethics and Economics of Suicide in Old Age."
- "Age-Rationing and the Just Distribution of Health Care: Is There a Duty to Die?"

Emanuel formerly chaired the United States Institute of Health's Department of Bioethics (i.e. euthanasia education) while also engineering the Complete Lives System. On January 31, Britain's leading medical journal, *The Lancet*, published the crux of his proposal:

When implemented, the complete lives system produces a priority curve on which individuals aged between roughly 15 and 40 years get the most substantial chance, whereas the youngest and oldest people get chances that are attenuated.

On July 30, Jim O'Neil of *Canada Free Press* even cited Emanuel's thoughts on the way in which physicians should engage in their practice. "Doctors take the Hippocratic Oath too seriously as an imperative to do everything for the patient regardless of the cost, or the effects on others." Stated differently, the elderly should simply die so as to not be a burden on others. These words draw us perilously close to the dystopian societies envisioned in movies such as *THX 1138* and *Soylent Green*.

With new strains of a swine flu on the horizon, and therefore threats of forced vaccinations, how close are we to mandatory sterilizations and the Rockefeller-funded eugenics of decades past? In Barack Obama's chamber of horrors, one variable has become abundantly clear: individuals are expendable, especially if they're newborns or senior citizens.

Obama & Company Target Internet

Originally published: September 21, 2009

"**B**arack Obama wants to shut down the Internet. He's becoming Big Brother." These types of accusations are plaguing the highly criticized Cybersecurity Act of 2009 (S.773), but when analyzing this pending legislation, one vital point must be recognized. At this juncture in time, the government absolutely cannot terminate the Internet for any extended duration. In other words, there's not a single switch that can be flipped to bring it all to a grinding halt.

The reason revolves around the fact that U.S. Internet Service Providers (ISPs) are independent entities and not state-owned under one umbrella as they are in countries such as China or North Korea. Therefore, anyone who says the government can shut down the Internet for inordinate amounts of time either doesn't under the Internet's dynamics, or is pushing a fear-based agenda.

STANDARDIZATION

The real cause for concern revolves around how the government wants to deal with privately owned ISPs. As it stands now, the Net is reminiscent of an unregulated Wild West frontier. But if President Obama were to declare a "cybersecurity emergency" under this newly updated legislation, our country's communications networks would actually become more vulnerable to external control.

In the Jay Rockefeller (D-W.V.) and Olivia Snowe (R-Maine) bill, federal authorities would create a single, standardized set of regulations for all designated private networks. The ramifications are obvious. Greg Nojeim of the Center for Democracy & Technology warned in April, "If everyone builds to the same standard and the bad guys know these standards, it makes it easier for the bad guys." Thus, rather than trying to cripple a very complex, autonomous worldwide web (a virtually impossible task), *Huliq News* points out, "Those attacking the U.S. could break through the single standard rather than the various ones that exist now."

COMPUTER CZAR

If a national emergency arises, Roy Marks wrote on August 31 in "Revised Bill Still Gives Obama Unprecedented Cyber-security Powers," "The secretary of commerce would have the authority to access 'all relevant data concerning [ISPs] without regard to any provision of law, regulation, rule or policy restricting such access.'" This agency, in league with the National Security Agency (NSA), will then decide when the Internet is to be restored following any given crisis situation.

Wayne Crews, technology director at the Competitive Enterprise Institute, states, "Virtually anything networked to some other computer is potentially fair game if President Obama exercises 'emergency powers.'" In the meantime, researcher and activist Tom Burghardt surmised on August 29 that the government and mainstream media will "become the sole conduit for critical news and information during a 'national emergency.'"

The ominous nature of this standardization (including "cybersecurity blacklists") is reflected in a commentary by techno-journalist Declan McCullagh. "If your company is deemed 'critical,' a new set of regulations kicks in involving who you can hire, what information you must disclose, and when the government would exercise control over your computers or network."

In their zeal to freeze private online service providers, Dwight Schwab, Jr., in "Still Think 'Big Brother' is a Silly Concept," notes that the heavy-handed actions mentioned earlier will ensue at the government's sole discretion via licensed "cybersecurity professionals."

Considering the recent spate of cyber attacks against our country, lawmakers should instead focus on strengthening the safety of their own networks. In addition, many Americans feel more threatened by the intrusiveness of their own government rather than the perpetual bogeymen used to keep us in a state of continual fear.

To augment this point, Burghardt examined the Cybersecurity Act's sponsors. "Drafted by Senators Jay Rockefeller and Olivia Snowe, 'best friends forever' of the National Security Agency and the telecommunications industry, they were the key enablers of Bush-era warrantless wiretapping and privacy-killing data mining programs that continue apace under Obama."

Burghardt continues, "*The New York Times* revealed in June how a former NSA analyst described a secret database code-named Pinwale that archived foreign and domestic e-mail messages . . . two intelligence officers confirmed that the program was still in operation." In a June 16 *New York Times* article by James Risen and Eric Lichblau, government officials testified before Congress that "intercepts of the private telephone calls and e-mail messages of Americans are broader than previously acknowledged."

Where the subject of computers is concerned, right now government officials are limited in their ability to shut down the Internet. But if draconian new legislation is passed, they will greatly increase their potential to make themselves the sole providers of information in times of widespread upheaval and panic. If such an apparatus is established, Americans may find themselves in a "virtual void" when information and technology is most needed.

BLACK PANTHER SUPPORTERS

Revolutionary Black Radicals Infest Washington, D.C.

Originally published: October 5, 2009

Say what you will about Sen. Joseph McCarthy, he was correct about one important fact—communists had infiltrated the U.S. government during the 1940s and 1950s. Likewise, when historians examine our current administration, their verdict will similarly be: that's when Marxists and black nationalists resurfaced, under President Obama.

Fortunately, one of these self-avowed communists—green jobs czar "Van" Jones—resigned amid a firestorm of controversy concerning past extremist statements.

A number of these are included below:

- Violence—"You never see a Columbine done by black children. It's only suburban white kids."
- When questioned about the GOP's former senate majority—"The answer to that is, they're a--holes."
- The Rodney King trial—"I was a rowdy nationalist on April 28, and then the verdicts came down on April 29. By August, I was a communist."
- Ghettos—"White polluters and white environmentalists are essentially steering poison into the people-of-color communities because they don't have a racial justice frame."
- Economics—"We want to move from suicidal gray capitalism to eco-capitalism."
- Political tactics—"I'm willing to forego the cheap satisfaction of the radical pose for the deep satisfaction of radical ends."

- Law and order—He's a supporter of cop killer Abu Mumia Jamal, whose adherents "likened supporters of murdered police officer Daniel Faulkner to the KKK."
- He named his son "Cabral" after South African Marxist revolutionary Amilcar Cabral, who by the way called Vladimir Lenin "the greatest champion of national liberation."
- President Bush—referred to him as a "crackhead licking the crack pipe for another fix."
- USA—Jones once attended a "Challenging White Supremacy Workshop" sponsored by Anti-Racism for Global Justice. In its own words, this group is committed to: multiculturalism, feminism, queer and transgender liberation and anti-capitalism.
- He helped form a group called STORM (Standing Together to Organize a Revolutionary Movement) that, by its own admission, bases itself on Marxism, Leninism and radical Maoism.
- Anarchy—"I met all these young radical people of color [in jail]—I mean really radical; communists and anarchists. And it was like, 'This is what I need to be part of.' I spent the next ten years of my life working with a lot of these people I met in jail, trying to be a revolutionary."

GREEN JOBS CZAR

In the guise of a "cleaner environment," Obama and his leftists have initiated an aggressive power grab to assume control of the U.S. government. According to Phil Kerpen, policy director of Americans for Prosperity, "The 'green jobs' concept is merely a new face on the old ideology of central economic planning and control, an alternative and a threat to free market capitalism."

As such, Van Jones and his ilk are promoting the enormously taxladen cap-and-trade program that will inevitably destroy our economy. But the entire concept is, in reality, an exercise in the redistribution of wealth. Kerpen rightly points out, "Green jobs are not economic jobs, but political jobs designed to funnel vast sums of taxpayer money to left-wing labor unions, environmental groups, and social justice community organizers."

SEPTEMBER 11

Despite his extreme perspectives, the pivotal act that led to Van Jones's dismissal from office was his signature on a 9-11 petition in 2004. Those in the 9-11 truth movement may consider Jones an ally, but once this document became public knowledge, he immediately disavowed 9-11 as an inside job or a pretext for war. Claiming that he didn't agree with the petition's stance, Jones stressed, "It certainly does not reflect my views, now or ever."

Writing for *Front Page* magazine on September 4, Ben Johnson commented, "On the evening after 9-11, Jones stood in the streets with the Maoist-communist organization he founded—STORM—to denounce the United States for having brought this disaster on itself." Even then, Jones had it wrong because U.S. citizens didn't cause these attacks; nor did they deserve them. Rather, Jones should have had the courage to paint an accurate picture—that 9-11 was a joint covert operation between Israeli intelligence forces and a cabal of Zionists within the U.S. government. But instead of telling the truth, Van Jones would rather promote a treasonous anti-American agenda spawned by Marxist black nationalists.

James O'Keefe and Hannah Giles dressed up like a pimp and a prostitute and entered several ACORN offices looking for help as to how best to set up a prostitution ring in public housing areas. In several instances, the ACORN employees offered advice how to make such a business thrive. At left, O'Keefe and Giles out of costume.

Obama & ACORN Falling Fast

Originally published: October 5, 2009

Dressed outlandishly as a pimp and prostitute, 25-year-old film-maker James O'Keefe and 20-year-old Hannah Giles strolled into a number of ACORN offices to see whether they could secure home loans to open a brothel. With a video camera in tow, the couple recorded their exploits in Baltimore, Washington D.C., Brooklyn and San Bernardino. The resulting footage has cast a harsh light on one of the most corrupt institutions in America—and one with direct ties to Barack Obama.

AIDING & ABETTING

Asked why they targeted ACORN, Giles replied matter-of-factly, "Because they're a thug organization getting my tax dollars." Her assessment rings true, for workers advised them on how to open a house of ill repute, launder their prostitution earnings through intermediaries, and avoid paying income taxes to the IRS. Employees also didn't bat an eye when told that the couple planned on importing 13-year-old Salvadoran illegal alien sex slaves to turn tricks. They were even told to list these underage girls as dependents if they did file tax returns (despite the implications of human smuggling and child prostitution).

Ms. Giles also learned that, when dealing with banks, she could fraudulently list her occupation as "freelance performing artist." One representative in California also bragged about "influence peddling" with local, state and federal officials in the Democratic Party.

When shown this damning evidence (complete with an inherent kickback scheme), Stuart Katzenberg—director of ACORN's Maryland branch—typically called it "racist."

CORRUPTION

ACORN received $53.6 million in federal tax dollars from 1994 to 2008, and was eligible for billions more in stimulus money. But the grifters in this intricately woven crime syndicate didn't stop at illegally securing home loans (a widespread practice that contributed greatly to the recent housing market collapse). They've also had thirty employees convicted in nine different states for voter fraud registration. Similarly, Stephanie Strom pointed out in *The New York Times* on July 9, 2008 that founder "Dale Rathke embezzled $1 million from ACORN and affiliated charitable organizations in 1999 and 2000."

Matthew Vadum described a second Rathke brother for *The American Spectator* on September 13. "ACORN founder Wade Rathke didn't have a problem with domestic terrorists trying to kill delegates at the Republican Party's national convention in 2008, according to former radical community organizer Brandon Darby. Rathke denounced him for breaking the radicals' rule of silence. In January, Rathke suggested that it's better to let innocents die than to squeal on your comrades in the struggle."

CONSEQUENCES

Outraged, the Senate voted 83 to 7 on September 14 to cut off all federal ACORN funding. The House followed on September 17. In addition, to eliminate potential gerrymandering in 2010, the U.S. Census Bureau severed all ties with ACORN because they "no longer have confidence that our national partnership agreement is being effectively managed through their local offices." Lastly, the Louisiana state attorney general, James Caldwell, has now issued a subpoena for ACORN's financial records, as well as those of Dale Rathke.

OBAMA'S CONNECTIONS

Although Barack Obama and his apologists are desperately trying to distance him from ACORN, they have deep and long-standing ties with this organization. It's even fair to say that Barack Obama equals ACORN. Consider that in 2008, the Obama campaign contributed $832,598 to ACORN for new voter registration. He also served as executive director of Project Value, ACORN's voter registration arm, in 1992. The following year, Obama acted as ACORN's attorney and sued the state of Illinois on its behalf to initiate a "motor voter" law.

As a board member of the Woods Fund and Joyce Foundation, Obama funneled enormous amounts of money to ACORN. Stanley Kurtz wrote in the *National Review* on May 29, 2008, "Obama's memberships on these foundation boards allowed him to help direct tens of millions of dollars in grants to various liberal organizations, including Chicago ACORN."

Obama's own words also illustrate the intimate link between him and these community organizers, many of whom share the radical philosophy of Chicago provocateur Saul Alinsky. Addressing ACORN leaders in November 2007, Obama declared, "I come out of a grassroots organizing background. . . . I've been fighting alongside ACORN on issues you care about my entire career. Even before I was an elected official, when I ran the Project Value registration in Illinois, ACORN was smack dab in the middle of it."

On December 1, 2007 at the Heartland Democratic Presidential Forum for ACORN and other community organizers, Obama promised, "Before I even get inaugurated, during the transition, I'm going to be calling all of you in to help us shape our agenda." He also told ACORN during his campaign that they would "have a seat at the table in my administration." Needless to say, ACORN endorsed Obama in the 2008 presidential race.

On May 18, Matthew Vadum revealed how the illegal financial ties between these two entities were suppressed last year. "*The New York Times* finally went on the record to admit that just before the election it killed a politically sensitive news story involving corruption allegations that might have made the Obama campaign look bad."

With public furor rising over this situation, Barack Obama should order the FBI and Attorney General Eric Holder to investigate ACORN to determine whether they violated any federal RICO statues. The protection racket has to end.

Rod Blagojevich's 'Bagman'
Dies Mysteriously

Originally published: October 5, 2009

When Bill and Hillary Clinton were co-governors and co-presidents, people kept dying around them, especially in Arkansas. Now that Barack Obama is commander-in-chief, people keep dying around him, especially in Chicago. There were the two choir members who attended Rev. Wright's church, Freddie Mac CFO David Kellermann, health consultant John Ruff who mysteriously died in a car crash, and now Rod Blagojevich's top advisor, Christopher Kelly.

Known as Blago's bagman, Kelly incurred huge debts to Barack Obama's bagman, convicted businessman Tony Rezko. Late on the evening of September 11, Kelly's mistress found him soaked in vomit inside his Cadillac Escalade, apparently from a "Tylenol overdose." Authorities later said rat poison might have been involved, while typically suggesting that he'd been suffering from "depression."

After being rushed to Oak Forest Hospital, physicians resuscitated their patient and stabilized him, as private detective Paul Huebl described. "Kelly was sitting up, lucid, while talking with medical providers and police."

However, after being transferred to Stroger Hospital 25 miles away, Kelly inexplicably died a few hours later at 10:46 Saturday morning. In the meantime, as Georgia Garvey and Antonion Olivio reported for the *Chicago Tribune* on September 14, "A 'mystery man' with gray hair unsuccessfully tried to pick up Kelly's SUV from the hospital with keys in hand." Police have yet to identify this "person of interest."

Kelly was set to begin an eight-year federal prison sentence for mail fraud and an $8.5 million kickback scheme at O'Hare International Airport. He also faced racketeering, fraud and extortion charges in the Blago case. In addition, authorities put intense pressure on Kelly to testify against those who orchestrated the pay-for-play scam to fill Barack Obama's vacant Senate seat. Freelance writer Gregory Tejeda of the *Chicago Argus* commented on September 14, "This was a 'murder' done for political cover to keep Kelly quiet and prevent other political people from being taken down by federal prosecutors."

America's First 'Jewish' President?

Originally published: October 12, 2009

On December 12, 2008 Abner Mikva, a Jewish former counsel member in the Clinton White House, quipped, "Barack Obama will go down in history as America's first Jewish president." Earlier last year, *The Wall Street Journal* ran an article on April 21 that included a quote from Judson Miner, a Jewish lawyer who gave Obama his first job in Chicago. "'I used to tease Barack that he had Jewish blood,' says Mr. Miner. The connections to Judaism run even closer to home: Michelle Obama's second cousin converted to Judaism, was ordained a rabbi and runs a Chicago congregation made up largely of black converts to Judaism."

Similarly, on April 16, 2008 the *L.A. Times* ran a headline, *Barack Obama Claims Jewish Kinship* after he told an audience, "My links to the Jewish community are not political. They preceded my entry into politics."

Previous chapters in this book have listed the number of individuals in Obama's inner circle who are Jewish. Likewise, Obama's closest confidant, Valerie Jarrett, is the protégé of Marilyn Katz, a Jewish security provider for the SDS (Students for a Democratic Society). According to scholar Arthur Liebman, 46 percent of all SDS delegates in the 1960s were Jewish, with five of nine presidents being Jewish.

Katz introduced Jarrett to Daniel Levin (Jewish), who gave her a real estate job, whereupon she worked with Obama's bagman, convicted felon Tony Rezko. Katz also founded the New American Movement (which included the Communist Party USA) with Rabbi Michael Lerner.

In regard to the president, one of Katz's clients, Project Vote (an ACORN affiliate), brought Obama to Chicago. She also introduced Obama at his first nationwide anti-war speech on October 2, 2002, then served on his finance committee and as a bundler during the 2008 presidential race.

Further, Katz has known Weather Underground terrorist William Ayers (a disciple of the SDS) for over forty years. Ayers is married to fellow Weather Underground member Bernadine Dohrn (Jewish), and served with Obama on the Woods Fund (which provided a major expansion in funding to ACORN). Ayers also arranged for Walter and Leonore Annenberg (Jewish) to name Obama the first chairman of the prestigious Annenberg Foundation in 1995.

Similarly, Valerie Jarrett's mother ran the Erickson Institute, where one of the board members was Tom Ayers, father of Bill Ayers. Bernadine Dohrn also served on this board.

Fellow Weather Underground founder Jeff Jones is married to Eleanor Stein (Jewish), and was credited by Senate Majority leader Harry Reid for writing most of the recent stimulus bill via the Apollo Alliance. Jones also served with Van Jones, a self-avowed communist, in this same organization.

Then, none other than Valerie Jarrett brought Van Jones into the Obama Cabinet. She boasted at the *Daily Kos* conference on August 15, "We have been watching Van Jones for some years and are so delighted to recruit him into the White House." In addition, Jarrett hired Michelle Robinson (Obama) in 1991 to work in Mayor Daley's office, then opened doors for the couple to enter Chicago's most liberal social circles.

Another influential member of Obama's cabinet with close ties to Jarrett is senior adviser David Axelrod (Jewish). Jarrett first hired him at the Urban Health Institute, and then longtime Democratic insider Betty Lu Saltzman (Jewish) introduced Axelrod to Obama in 1992.

Axelrod's two mentors were journalist/activists Don Rose and David S. Canter, both Jewish. Rose held membership in a Communist Party organization labeled the Alliance to End Repression, while their president and directors were Richard Criley, Abe Feinglass, Jack Spiegel and Norman Roth, all Jewish. Rose also knew Marilyn Katz quite well through the SDS, and the newspaper he owned pushed Marxist causes while also promoting Abner Mikva, one of Obama's early Jewish mentors. Not to be outdone, his partner's father, Harry J. Canter, acted as secretary of Boston's Communist Party.

The extent of this collaboration between various questionable factions in Chicago is reflected in the comments of Rabbi Arnold Wolf, a Democratic socialist. "We had a party for [Obama] at our house when he was just starting back in the nineties. I said right away: here's a guy who could sell our product, and sell it with splendor!"

In-depth research done on Barack Obama during the past few years proves that his rise to power can be unequivocally mapped as follows. At the top exist extremely wealthy Jewish financiers such as the Rothschilds and George Soros, who've set his course in motion. To carry out this plan are mid-level Jewish operatives (Rahm Emanuel, Axelrod, Bernanke, Summers, Katz etc), along with hard-line Marxist sympathizers. Lastly, at the street level are a host of black nationalists such as Van Jones and Rev. Wright whose rhetoric is aggressively anti-white. Toss in a very pro-Obama Jewish-controlled media, and it's ultimately clear how he reached the Oval Office at 1600 Pennsylvania Avenue.

YOUNG BARACK OBAMA AND HIS MOTHER, STANLEY ANN DUNHAM

Who Is Barack Obama's Real Father?

Originally published: October 19, 2009

Has the Obama birth certificate debate been a deliberate distraction to divert attention away from an even more crucial issue— the identity of his real father? In a Sept. 26 interview, journalist and Illinois senatorial candidate Andy Martin theorized that communist poet Frank Marshall Davis may actually be the man who sired Obama, and that this event is the foundation for his later rise in politics.

FRANK MARSHALL DAVIS

Born in Kansas in 1905, Davis relocated to Chicago in 1927, where he spent the next 21 years. Before moving to Hawaii in 1948, it's reported that Davis also landed in Seattle. Barack Obama's grandparents were originally from Kansas (where they knew Davis), and also migrated to Seattle. In 1960, the family uprooted again to Hawaii, whereupon they renewed ties with Davis. Prior to reaching Honolulu, Davis married a white Chicago socialite named Helen Canfield in 1946. Both were members of the American Communist Party (CPUSA), which was founded in Chicago in 1919. His involvement with communism, dating back to 1931, became so pronounced that in 1951 the House Un-American Activities Committee accused him of involvement in the CPUSA.

As a columnist for numerous Red-leaning publications, Davis potentially filled another role. As Niall Kilkenny of *Reformation Online* reports, "Sometime between 1927 and 1948, Frank Marshall Davis was recruited as a special agent or informer for the FBI. As a newspaperman, Davis had the perfect opportunity to know what was happening in Chicago. As a left wing or 'communist' sympathizer, no one would suspect him of associating with the ultra-right-wing FBI."

THE DUNHAM FAMILY

In 1955, Obama's grandparents and mother migrated to Seattle, where they specifically enrolled their daughter in Mercer Island High School. Again, a troubling element arises. According to Tim Jones of *The Chicago Tribune* on March 27, 2007, "In 1955, the chairman of the Mercer Island school board, John Stenhouse, testified before the House Un-American Activities Committee that he had been a member of the Communist Party." Described as a "full-fledged radical leftist" upon graduating high school, Ann Dunham followed her parents to Hawaii in 1960. Classmate Susan Blake described her as someone who "never dated crew-cut white boys." Her father Stanley was also non-conventional, drinking whiskey, smoking marijuana and chasing women in Honolulu's red-light district with Frank Marshall Davis.

SEX REBEL

In 1968, San Diego's Greenleaf Classics published a book entitled *Sex Rebel: Black* by "Bob Greene." Years later, Frank Marshall Davis admitted to authoring the book under a pseudonym. In this autobiographical tome, Davis proclaims himself to be bisexual, a voyeur, exhibitionist, mildly interested in sadomasochism and deriving sexual gratification (he claims in the book) from "simulated rape and [flogging]." Davis also wrote in the book's introduction that although he "changed names and identities, all incidents I described have been taken from actual experiences."

Even creepier, Davis recounts an incident of "swinging" with a couple from Seattle, and how he and his wife had numerous encounters with an underage girl named "Anne." He confessed, "I'm not one to go for 'Lolitas'. Usually I'd rather not bed a babe under 20. But there are exceptions." Obama's grandparents lived in Seattle, knew Davis well, and his mother's name was Ann. There also exist three different nude pictures of Obama's mother that were allegedly taken at Frank Marshall Davis's apartment. Davis was, in addition to being a journalist, an amateur photographer.

FATHER CONTROVERSY

According to Barack Obama's official biography, his mother became impregnated by Barack Obama, Sr. in November 1960, and married the Kenyan in February 1961. But Andy Martin, known as the man who "gave birth to the birthers movement," claims Frank Marshall Davis sired Ann Durham's child, then paid off a Hawaii University student named Barack Obama to take responsibility.

The reasoning behind this argument is as follows: Davis was already married to a wealthy white socialite who would not have looked kindly on him impregnating an eighteen-year-old girl. By agreeing to this arrangement and marrying Dunham, Barack Obama Sr. could legally stay in the U.S. Obama would not have taken his new family back to Kenya because he already had a wife and two other children there. Plus, his father disapproved of his marriage to Dunham.

Dunham and Obama never lived together after their marriage and never shared the same address. In fact, almost immediately after Obama's birth, Dunham moved to Washington State, while Obama Sr. relocated to Harvard a year later.

Obama Jr. spent much of his youth apart from his mother, who lived in Indonesia or the U.S. During this time, his grandparents raised him, while also maintaining a close relationship with Frank Marshall Davis.

Did Ann Dunham justify leaving her son because his real father was still nearby? In his autobiography, *Dreams From My Father*, Barack Obama describes Davis as a "father figure" and mentor. Also, prior to his enrollment in college, he penned a poem about Davis entitled *Pop*.

Whenever Obama needed counseling during his teen years, the grandparents invariably went to Davis to provide advice.

An even more bizarre notion arises from well-known author Jerome Corsi, whose October 30, 2008 article *Marxist "Mentor" Sold Drugs with Obama*, carried the following lines: "Obama was a young kid, about 14 or 15 years old. I was told his name was Barry, and there was no doubt Barry knew Davis was selling marijuana and cocaine as well as hot dogs from his hot dog stand. Barry was also there with an older white gentleman I'm told was Stanley." Obama revealed his marijuana and cocaine use in *Dreams From My Father*, while his grandfather's name was Stanley.

OBAMA'S CAREER

As a virulent racist, Davis sent Obama off to college with the following words: "You're not going to college to get educated. You're going to get trained. You may be a well-trained, well-paid nigger, but you're a nigger just the same." Does this "sage advice" now explain how Obama and Michelle gravitated to the anti-white preaching of Rev. Jeremiah Wright?

At Occidental College in Los Angeles, Obama describes hanging out with "Marxist philosophers" and attending "socialist conferences." In the meantime, his mother found employment with USAID and the Ford Foundation, both of which served as fronts for the CIA and Rockefeller Foundation. In 1981, Obama—supposedly a poor college student from a broken home abandoned by both parents—traveled to Indonesia, Pakistan and India. Numerous investigators have postulated that the CIA funded these trips. Also, according to Don Frederick's well-researched timeline, while in Pakistan, Obama's host, Muhammadian Soomro, was linked to the notorious Bank of Credit and Commerce International (BCCI), which was involved in "money laundering, bribery, terrorist support, tax evasion, smuggling and illegal immigration." They also worked very closely with the CIA.

Upon returning to the U.S. in 1981, Obama's next destination was New York City and Columbia University. Again, where did he obtain the money to attend an Ivy League college? According to his official biography, Obama graduated from Columbia in 1983. But something strange arises from this time period. When questioned by *The New York Times* about his undergraduate studies, Obama "declined repeated requests to talk about his New York years, release his Columbia transcripts, or identify even a single fellow student, co-worker, roommate or friend from those years."

Further, there are no pictures of him in the Columbia yearbook, and Fox News contacted 400 students from that era, none of whom remembered Obama. Wayne Allyn Root, Libertarian vice presidential candidate in 2008, was—like Obama—a political science major at Columbia who graduated in 1983 (purportedly the same year as Obama). Root makes a startling disclosure. "I don't know a single person at Columbia that knows him, and they all know me. I don't have a classmate who ever knew Barack Obama at Columbia. Ever! Nobody recalls him. I'm not exaggerating. Class of '83 political science, pre-law. You don't get more exact than that. I don't know anyone who ever met him there. Is that not strange?"

As a result, Obama's college records and transcripts from Occidental, Columbia and Harvard have all been sealed and not released—just like his "official" birth certificate has been sealed and not released by Hawaii's governor.

WILLIAM AYERS

What we do know about Obama's tenure at Columbia is that he lived only a few blocks away from Weather Underground terrorist William Ayers, and that both attended socialist meetings at Cooper Union during the early 1980s. More importantly, Frank Marshall Davis was a close friend of Ayers's father, Thomas, in Chicago, and purportedly arranged for Obama to meet William Ayers via his arrival in New York City. Even wilder is the fact that Obama also met and was tutored by Zbigniew Brzezinski during this time. Brzezinski is a perennial Bilderberg attendee, as well as CFR member and co-founder of the Trilateral Commission with David Rockefeller. Now, how often does a poor college kid from a broken family get to be mentored by one of the most powerful men in the world? Brzezinski eventually became one of the first people to endorse Obama's candidacy, then served as his foreign policy advisor during the campaign.

During the interim between Columbia and his pilgrimage to Chicago, Obama worked for the Business International Corporation, a CIA-front that specialized in recruiting left-wing organizers to use as assets. The similarities between his early college days and those of another CIA plant—Bill Clinton—are remarkable.

But if we return to William Ayers, an even more crucial element appears. In a recent book entitled *Barack and Michelle*, best-selling author Christopher Andersen contends that Ayers is actually the author of Obama's *Dreams From My Father*. He posits, "The book's language, oddly specific references, literary devices and themes bear a jarring similarity to Ayers's own writing."

There's more. Obama met his wife at the Chicago law firm of Sidley Austin, where Valerie Jarrett hired her. One of this firm's major clients was Tom Ayers (father of Bill Ayers), while Michelle's mentor was Bernadine Dohrn (wife of Bill Ayers).

Then, Obama kicked off his political career with a fundraiser at the home of none other than William Ayers and Bernadine Dohrn. There, Illinois Senator Alice Palmer announced that she was stepping down from her post and hand-selected Obama as her successor. In *The Case Against Barack Obama*, researcher David Freddoso alleges that Palmer "was identified by the FBI as being on the Soviet payroll in the eighties and an enthusiastic attendee of the 27th Congress of the Communist Party."

VALERIE JARRETT

Most recently, a woman named Valerie Jarrett has been described as Barack Obama's "eyes and ears," "the other side of Obama's brain," "Obama's political godmother," "Michelle and Barack's consigliere," plus "Obama's alter-ego and inner conscience." Those in the know say the Obamas don't make a move without her input, and that she provides street credibility to the radical black community. During the Obamas August vacation in Massachusetts, they visited her home, while a Chicago political insider describes Jarrett thusly: "She knows where all the bodies have been buried in the past 30 or so years of Chicago politics, and she knows all the tricks. If Obama had a political and financial godmother, it would be Valerie."

Obama has stated, "I trust her [Jarrett] completely to speak for me, particularly when we're dealing with delicate issues." As a "fixer" par excellence, Jarrett suggests, "We have a kind of mind meld."

What makes Jarrett so influential? Her father-in-law—Vernon Jarrett—worked at the same communist-leaning newspaper—*The Chicago Defender*—as did Frank Marshall Davis. They were also close associates in Chicago's CPUSA, as well as belonging to a variety of other communist organizations.

Vernon Jarrett then went on to become *The Chicago Tribune's* first black writer, in addition to founding the National Association of Black Journalists. In this capacity, Jarrett used his clout to help Harold Washington become Chicago's first black mayor. Then, after landing an assignment at *The Chicago Sun-Times*, Jarrett used his columns to help promote an up-and-coming superstar, Barack Obama.

On top of that, Valerie Jarrett's great-uncle is none other than longtime Bilderberg member Vernon Jordan (Bill and Hillary Clinton's "fixer"). Her ties go even deeper. Jarrett's mother, Barbara Taylor Bowman, appointed Tom Ayers—William Ayers father—to the Erickson Group's board of trustees.

Subsequently, Jarrett hired Michelle Robinson (Obama) to work for Mayor Daley's political machine and is also cited as the reason why Barack moved to Chicago. In this sense, one of Davis's associates—William Ayers—drew Obama to Chicago from one end, while another Davis connection—Valerie Jarrett—drew Michelle in from the other. Again, the similarities between Bill and Hillary Clinton's "prearranged relationship" cannot be denied.

Jarrett also had close ties with fellow slumlord Tony Rezko (Obama's bagman), and was the person first mentioned to fill Obama's vacant Senate seat (leading to the Blago pay-to-play scandal). *Judicial Watch* lists her as one of the nation's top ten most corrupt politicians, and it is she who traveled to Copenhagen with Michelle Obama to make a final bid for Chicago to be the Olympic host city in 2016. Lastly, Jarrett brought self-avowed communist Van Jones in as the green jobs czar, while also completing Obama's inner circle with David Axelrod, Rahm Emanuel and company.

In the end, this article by no means proves that Frank Marshall Davis is Barack Obama's father, any more than other stories that allege Malcolm X sired him. Without an original birth certificate, speculation will obviously continue. However, Frank Marshall Davis cultivated all of the above-mentioned Chicago roots back in the early 1920s. As a pivotal figure in the Communist Party's inception, his deep-seated connections in the Windy City certainly must be considered when viewing Barack Obama's startling rise to the presidency in 2008.

JOE McCARTHY: PROVEN RIGHT—AGAIN?

Obama Surrounded by Real, Live 21st Century Communists

Originally published: November 30, 2009

From the end of WWII until the Soviet Union fell in 1991, America's foreign policy revolved around fighting communism. Yet during the past decade, a plethora of self-avowed communists and Marxist sympathizers have clustered around President Barack Obama.

In June, White House Communications Director Anita Dunn told a St. Andrews high school graduating class, "Two of my favorite political philosophers are Mao Tse-tung and Mother Teresa." Similarly, Manufacturing Czar Ron Bloom informed the 2008 Union League Club, "We know that the free market is nonsense. We kind of agree with Mao that political power comes largely from the barrel of a gun."

Energy czar Carol Browner belonged to the Commission for a Sustainable World Society (a group run by the Socialists International). On the other hand, long-time friend William Ayers admitted in 1995, "Maybe I'm the last communist who is willing to admit it: The ethics of communism still appeal to me." Communist-leaning journalist Don Rose mentored Chief of Staff David Axelrod, whereas rumored Obama father Frank Marshall Davis belonged to the Communist Party since the early 1920s.

During a September 17 speech, spiritual advisor Jeremiah Wright praised "no-nonsense Marxism," net neutrality proponent Robert McChesney wrote about "a broader struggle for socialism" in 2000, while science czar John Holdren seeks "de-development via redistribution of wealth." Finally, FCC diversity czar Mark Lloyd recently lauded Hugo Chavez's socialist revolution as "incredible," whereas regulator czar Cass Sunstein championed one of the basic tenets of the *Communist Manifesto* in 1999 by declaring, "Without taxes, there would be no liberty."

It's now been proven that the vast majority of those behind Russia's Bolshevik Revolution were Jewish. Likewise, a significant number of Barack Obama's closest financiers, advisors and Cabinet members have been Jewish ever since his political career began. In this vein, scholar Eliot Ratzman noted, "In the 20th century, most Jews aligned themselves to three major versions of 'utopia': Jewish nationalism (Zionism), universalist socialism (communism), and liberal democracy (America)." Are the Marxists and Zionists surrounding Barack Obama merely a coincidence, or the result of a well-founded plot that has Senator Joe McCarthy rolling in his grave?

Obama 'Gay Accuser' Running For Congress

Originally published: December 21, 2009

By his own admission, Larry Sinclair is a convicted felon. He's served three stints in prison and is openly gay. He's also Barack Obama's worst nightmare, and in 2010 he's running for Congress in Florida's 24th district. His campaign slogan: "I have served my time; now it's time I serve my country."

Sinclair rose to prominence in January 2008 after releasing a *YouTube* video where, on November 6 and 7, 1999 he claims to have engaged in homosexual acts with then-Illinois Senator Barack Obama. During these trysts Sinclair alleges that he not only procured cocaine for Obama, but also smoked crack cocaine while engaging in sexual activity with the future president. Although relatively unknown outside his home state at the time, Obama hit the national stage in 2004 by delivering a keynote speech at the Democratic National Convention. Sinclair realized only then that he'd engaged in sex with an up-and-coming political superstar.

After hearing what he perceived to be blatant lies about Obama's sexuality and drug use, Sinclair uploaded his infamous *YouTube* video, made a television appearance in Puerto Rico, and addressed the National Press Club in Washington, D.C. on June 18, 2008. As a result, he describes in his book, *Barack Obama & Larry Sinclair: Coke, Sex, Lies & Murder,* how Senior Advisor David Axelrod spearheaded a vindictive smear campaign against him, while Sen. Joe Biden and his son Beau arranged for his arrest after the NPC speech. Even more incriminating, Sinclair writes about his concerns that Obama and Rev. Jeremiah Wright were involved in the murder of Obama's former lover, choirmaster Donald Young.

Many people will ask: why should we believe Sinclair's claims? Well, one of these individuals—President Obama—is pathologically evasive about his past, while the other reveals himself with candid frankness, warts and all. Considering the enormous amounts of controversy he faces, why doesn't our commander-in-chief simply exhibit the unprecedented transparency he promised during his 2008 campaign? To date, Barack Obama's college records and transcripts from Occidental, Columbia and Harvard have all been sealed and not released—just like his "official" birth certificate has been sealed and not released by Hawaii's governor. Similarly shrouded in secrecy are his medical records, college thesis, University of Chicago articles, Illinois State Senatorial files, hospital birth records, passport, parents' marriage license and past relationships with terrorist William Ayers and ACORN. Who is Barack Obama? More importantly, why does his habitual lack of candor make it appear as if he has something to hide?

To support his claims, Sinclair provides hotel and limousine receipts from that time period, in addition to providing the name of his driver and the company that provided transportation services. On the other hand, Obama has submitted no public records of his whereabouts on the two dates in question, or any proof of an alibi that he wasn't in Chicago that weekend. If Sinclair were attempting to pull a scam, why is he so specific about the details? All the Obama camp has to do is disprove one tiny fact and Sinclair's entire story is undermined.

Plus, rather than claiming they were together only once, Sinclair doubles the odds by saying they were lovers on two successive days. Think how much easier it would have been for Sinclair to simply say their tryst occurred "sometime in November 1999." Further, Obama has admitted to cocaine use in the past, as did his "father-figure/mentor" in Hawaii, Frank Marshall Davis, who wrote of his own bisexuality in the book *Sex Rebel: Black*. Sinclair could have also easily claimed that Obama merely snorted cocaine; but instead, he upped the ante by pointing out his "lover" smoked crack.

Speaking of Davis, a Windy City resident for two decades and an early gay rights advocate, it seems that Chicago's South Side has historically harbored a flourishing underground gay community—one of the nation's first—long before San Francisco established itself in a similar fashion. Oddly enough, Obama selected this very South Side of Chicago—over any other locale in America—to begin his political career. The person who opened doors for Obama was none other than "spiritual mentor" Rev. Wright, whose

South Side church welcomes gays and lesbians, and performs same-sex marriages. The circle widens when we consider William Ayers—the man who hosted Obama's first fundraiser—who wrote in his biography, *Fugitive Days*, of being sexual partners "with his best male friend." Ayers also served as ghostwriter for Obama's biography, *Dreams From My Father*.

In his recently released book, Sinclair also asks: why was Donald Young, the openly gay choirmaster at Rev. Jeremiah Wright's Trinity United Church of Christ, murdered? More importantly, according to Sinclair, Young told him, "Barack and I have been lovers for some time and Rev. Wright knows it." Prior to being killed, how did Young—who had never met Larry Sinclair—obtain four different phone numbers belonging to the author? Sinclair tells his readers that Young confessed that Sen. Obama provided them to him.

If, indeed, Young and Obama were intimate, could his murder have been committed in order to silence the 47-year-old man? Larry Sinclair is easily discredited due to his checkered past. But if a second individual surfaced—like Donald Young, who also taught grade school mathematics and was highly respected within the church—and revealed his homosexual involvement with Obama, this development would be much more difficult to explain. Circumstances become even stranger. Although Young wasn't officially declared dead until 12:10 Sunday afternoon on December 23, 2007, Rev. Wright announced his death to parishioners Sunday morning. Further, although the cause of death had not yet been declared, Wright told his church that Young had been murdered.

How could he have known?

In the end, all of these suspicions could quickly be dismissed if Obama simply provided phone records from two time periods: (1) November 6 to 7, 1999 to disprove the illicit meeting with Larry Sinclair, and (2) September 2007 to December 2008 to dispel notions that he had extended contacts with Donald Young. On the other hand, Sinclair writes in his book, "*Chicago Tribune* reporter John Crewdson verified I indeed was in the Chicago area during the period stated of November 3, 1999 through November 8, 1999, and that I attended a Basic Training Graduation at the Great Lakes Navy Training Center."

Larry Sinclair is no angel, but his open past stands in stark contrast to Barack Obama, who remains huddled in a cocoon of secrecy that more and more people are beginning to question.

LARRY SINCLAIR'S WARNINGS ABOUT MICHELLE OBAMA

During a November 28 interview, Larry Sinclair warned, "Michelle Obama is who people need to be worried about. She's the one who groomed Obama. He didn't have any street smarts. He grew up around white people in Hawaii. He's never been black. It took Michelle and Rev. Wright to turn him black. South Chicago didn't originally embrace him. He's as lily white as you can get. Obama played the black community just like everyone else. The only time he's black is when he screws up and gets caught. That's when he plays the race card. Michelle equals his Chicago connection. She worked for Mayor Daley and introduced Obama to Bill Ayers and Bernadine Dohrn. Plus, Michelle's father was a streetwise union worker who knew the 'hood. Michelle is calling the shots in that house, and she sees Obama as a way to get what she wants."

I then asked Sinclair to describe how he perceived Obama in 1999. He responded, "Obama was a smooth hustler who'd go to bed with anybody if he saw the other person paying his way. That's why everyone needs to be concerned about the blackmail angle. Look at what happened to New Jersey Governor James McGreevey and his sex scandal with an Israeli intelligence officer."

THE TRUTH BEHIND JESSE JACKSON'S 'FREUDIAN SLIP'

When Jesse Jackson appeared on Fox News (July 9, 2008), he made a derogatory comment that had newscasts buzzing for days. With his microphone still hot, the "reverend" commented on Obama. "I wanna cut his nuts out." What the network didn't include (by their own admission) were other remarks uttered by the Chicago shakedown artist. Radio talk show host James Mtume claimed on "good authority" that Jackson also called Obama a "no good half-breed nigger." The big question is: what so upset Jackson? Well, three weeks earlier, Obama addressed a church congregation on Chicago's South Side and slammed black husbands and fathers as being "missing in action and AWOL." Were Jackson's extreme criticisms and bizarre references to castration a reflection of the hypocrisy that he and others in Chicago have observed, especially in regard to Obama's closeted sexuality, i.e. the pot calling the kettle black?

AFTERWORD:

Guilt by Association

I believe in guilt by association, especially if there is such a preponderance of evidence that no reasonable person could deny the implications. In the pages of this short book, I've presented an overwhelming amount of evidence linking Barack Obama to some of the most dangerous individuals this country has ever witnessed. Reminiscent of Richard Nixon's Plumbers, George Bush Sr.'s vast Iran-Contra criminal network, Bill and Hillary's Dixie Mafia and Dick Cheney's neo-con 9-11 killers, this president has spent a lifetime surrounding himself with an array of diabolical characters. Beginning with his childhood mentor (and some say father), Communist Party member Frank Marshall Davis, he continued to gravitate toward those whose goal has been the subversion of what most everyday citizens would consider American ideals. These men and women intend to destroy our great nation by demeaning us to some sort of afterthought in their grand Marxist experiment.

Particularly troublesome is how little people knew about Obama when selecting him to be their president. Even now, after reading quite possibly the most comprehensive portrait ever compiled on this man, he still remains an enigma. Manufactured to be elusive and trained in the fine art of subterfuge, Obama dodges the particulars of his life with amazing agility. His birthplace, birth certificate, father, travels, college transcripts, finances and colleagues all remain shrouded in mystery.

Worse, Obama and his handlers do everything possible to perpetuate this situation, knowing full well that exposure would sink this prized investment. As such, their innate sneakiness prompts one to continually wonder: what are they trying to hide? Moreover, by the time we find out, will it be too late for the fate of our country? Those who plot destruction never lay bare their intentions. Instead, they conceal them, as they do their very identity. The two act hand-in-hand with one another—concealed, lurking, plotting.

Those with eyes to see have noticed the elite Jewish financiers, the ever-present communist influence and the race-baiting black nationalists that surround Obama. They've molded him and led him to our nation's highest throne. And there he sits—reigning over the legions that have been duped.

Obama thrives on chicanery, deceit and misdirection. He wants us under his sway. Dependence becomes imprisonment, and as our sovereign self-reliance is replaced by the coming presence of totalitarianism, we'll end up bankrupted—financially, mentally and spiritually.

With this notion in mind, one final undeniable question must be asked: Are we content to simply be cogs in a deteriorating, collectivist-state envisioned by Barack Obama and his architects, or is the pursuit of individual freedom infinitely more valuable to us as human beings? The choice is clear: enslavement versus liberation.

—VICTOR THORN
May 2010

About the Author

VICTOR THORN founded Sisyphus Press in the fall of 2000 and is the author of 12 major books, as well as 10 chap books. He has published the works of numerous writers in the alternative media and has also produced four CD-ROMs and DVDs, including *Evidence of Revision*. Thorn is also the editor of four anthologies, and his political articles have appeared in various newspapers and magazines around the country. He was also co-host of *The Victor Thorn Show* on the Reality Radio Network from 2002 to 2003. In February 2004 he co-founded WING TV (World Independent News Group), which was a daily Internet television and radio talk show which was viewed in over 100 countries. Thorn has made hundreds of different radio and television appearances (including *Coast-to-Coast AM*, *The Lionel Show* on WOR 710), and has done a weekly one-hour news update on Alex Merklinger's *Mysteries of the Mind*, while also appearing weekly on Vyzygoth's *From the Grassy Knoll* radio show and Frank Whalen's *Frankly Speaking Radio*. Thorn has been an avid political activist who spoke at the OKC Bombing 10th anniversary, as well as protesting 9-11 in New York City and in front of the White House.

FRONTMAN

OBAMA'S DARKEST SECRETS REVEALED

In 2008, Barack Obama became the face of hope and change. Yet lurking behind the scenes is a host of personages who long ago selected this man to forward their global agenda. *Frontman* reveals the actual powers behind his throne: Bilderberg plotters, Zionist handlers, global financiers and Marxist activists.

Critics have called Obama an empty suit, but in actuality, the suit is filled by a cabal of men and women whose primary goal is to radically transform the United States. To cover their tracks, an air of secrecy has enveloped Obama's past, including his birth records, college transcripts and employment history.

While other books merely scratch the surface, *Frontman* tears away the deceptive smoke and mirrors that have been used to propel him into the Oval Office. By far the most comprehensive expose to date, President Barack Obama can no longer hide behind a façade that had been carefully created and orchestrated over the past few decades by people who are still pulling his strings. The title says it all: America's commander-in-chief is merely a figurehead for much more powerful people and forces.

Now, at long last, one of the most brutally honest portraits ever presented shows how our nation is being controlled by unseen hands that are leading us perilously close to disaster.

FRONTMAN: Softcover, 112 pages, #O, $20. Available from AMERICAN FREE PRESS, 645 Pennsylvania Avenue SE, #100, Washington, D.C. 20003. No charge for S&H inside the U.S. Call 1-888-699-6397 toll free to charge.

Books & Videos on 9-11

DVD: *9/11: The Myth & the Reality: A Devastating Exposé of the Myths and Lies About 9-11.* Double-DVD offers an account of 9-11 that is far more logical than the official federal version. Features Dr. David Ray Griffin—a cutting edge 9-11 researcher. Two bonus films included. Special features, two DVDs, over 3.5 hours, #MR, $30.

Debunking 9-11. Commentaries from William Rodriguez and Ellen Mariani, renowned columnist Paul Craig Roberts, Col. Donn de Grand Pré, Victor Thorn and more. Also all of AFP's groundbreaking coverage from the day 9-11 happened. More than 80 photographs. 8.5 x 11 format, color cover, 108 pages, #DE, $20. Published by AFP.

9-11 Evil: Israel's Central Role in the 9-11 Terror Attacks. Victor Thorn's blockbuster blows the lid off the media suppression of Israeli involvement in 9-11. Softcover, 123 pages, #E, $15.

9-11 on Trial: The World Trade Center Collapse. What caused the collapse of the three buildings of the WTC on 9-11? Is the establishment account credible? Victor Thorn puts the Bush theory of what happened on trial. Softcover, 175 pages, #911T, $14.

9-11 Exposed. A shocking 48-page booklet that attacks the federal fairy tale, explaining the 9-11 attacks with science. Demonstrates jet fuel can't melt construction-grade steel; bombs were in the Trade Center. Reveals: the pre-9-11 WTC "Power-Down"; 9-11 vacancies and absenteeism etc. Softcover booklet, 48 pages, #911EX, $8 each.

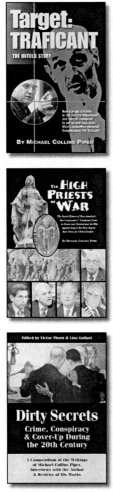

TARGET TRAFICANT: The Outrageous Story of How the Justice Department, the Israeli Lobby and the American Mass Media Conspired to Set Up and Take Down Congressman Jim Traficant—by Michael Collins Piper. The Traficant case is the most outrageous hit-and-run operation ever orchestrated against a U.S. public official. Piper dissects the intrigues of the Justice Department and the FBI and shows that the congressman was innocent of all of the charges. **Softcover, 176 pages, $25.**

THE HIGH PRIESTS OF WAR: The Secret History of America's Neo-Cons—The High Priests of War, by Michael Collins Piper, tells the secret history of how America's neo-conservatives came to power and orchestrated the war against Iraq as the first step in their drive for global power. Softcover, 144 pages, $20.

DIRTY SECRETS: Crime, Conspiracy & Cover-Up During the 20th Century—Here's a fascinating collection of writings from Michael Collins Piper, transcripts of uncensored radio interviews and reviews of his works—all compiled in one volume. Read where Piper's investigations have led him on such explosive topics as the Martin Luther King and JFK assassinations, the Oklahoma City bombing, the attack on the *Liberty* and many more. Softcover, 256 pages, $22.

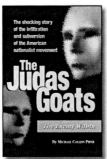

THE JUDAS GOATS: The Shocking Never-Before-Told Story of the Infiltration and Subversion of the American Nationalist Movement—BY MICHAEL COLLINS PIPER—Here is a detailed overview of the intrigues of the infamous Anti-Defamation League of B'nai B'rith, the corruption of the FBI and the CIA by Zionist elements, the evidence pointing toward Israeli involvement in the OKC bombing, the strange, little-known story of how Trotskyites seized command of the American "conservative" movement and also played a role in manipulating Sen. Joseph R. McCarthy's hunt for communists. Softcover, 376 pages, $25 per copy.

THE NEW JERUSALEM: Zionist Power in America—This explosive study contains all of the solid facts and figures documenting the massive accumulation of wealth and power by those who have used that influence to direct the course of American affairs—the forces behind America's "New Imperialism." While there are many historical books on "the Israeli lobby," this is unique. Another classic by Michael Collins Piper. Softcover, 184 pages, $20.

FUTURE FASTFORWARD: The Zionist Anglo-American Empire Meltdown—Is global "Empire Capitalism" about to come crashing down? Will there be a worldwide "people's war" against the Zionists and their powerful minions? Is nuclear war inevitable? What retribution will be meted out to those people who have foisted New World Order slavery upon the people of the world? By Asian political figure Matthias Chang. Softcover, 400 pages, $25. LIMITED QTY.

BRAINWASHED FOR WAR: Programmed to Kill—From the Cold War to Vietnam and now the so-called "War Against Terror" we have been lied to, mind-controlled and duped by a power elite with the goal of making us mindless supporters of bloody war. Also by Matthias Chang. Softcover, 556 pages, $30. LIMITED QTY. Call for availability.

NO BEAUTY IN THE BEAST: Israel Without Her Mascara—Author Mark Glenn examines Israel from a politically incorrect perspective and comes to the conclusion that the beast of John's Revelation is in fact the beast of Zionist supremacy—a beast that is now devouring the world. Also an amazing chapter of quotes from the perpetrators themselves. Must read for all who call themselves Christians. Softcover, 302 pages, $25.

ORDER ANY OR ALL of these books from AMERICAN FREE PRESS, 645 Pennsylvania Avenue SE, #100, Washington, D.C. 20003. To charge to Visa or MasterCard by phone, call 1-888-699-NEWS toll free.

WHAT REALLY HAPPENED

The official story of the Sept. 11, 2001 attacks on the United States is well known to most Americans. According to the U.S. government and the mainstream media, a group of 19 members of al Qaeda, a Muslim group led by Osama bin Laden, hijacked four U.S. airliners. Three were flown into buildings (the World Trade Center North and South towers and the Pentagon), and one crashed in Pennsylvania after a heroic effort by the passengers to regain control of the plane. That's the federal story.

But what facts are there to support this official scenario? As there was no debris from any airliner found at the Pentagon or at Shanksville, there is little to back up the claims there. And although most people will admit planes hit the World Trade Center towers, it is the strange collapse of those buildings and another massive skyscraper nearby that still confounds researchers and 9/11 skeptics.

In *9/11: What Really Happened*, Ed Whitney (author of *The Controllers: The Secret Rulers of the World*) explains what did and did not happen and presents a much more plausible scenario. In the end, Whitney convinces readers that the truth, in the case of 9/11, has been carefully kept from the U.S. public for nefarious reasons. Unlike other books, this one gives you what most likely happened.

Softcover, booklet, saddle-stitched, 61 pages, $10. Free S&H in U.S. Bulk prices: 1-9 copies are $10 each; 10-49 copies are $7.50 each. 50 or more are reduced to just $5 each.

Order from AMERICAN FREE PRESS, 645 Pennsylvania Avenue SE, #100, Washington, D.C. 20003. Call toll free 1-888-699-NEWS to charge.

In the maverick tradition of one of the great historians of the modern era . . .

No topic is "too controversial" for THE BARNES REVIEW, the most interesting history magazine published anywhere today. Commemorating the trailblazing path of the towering 20th Century revisionist historian, the late Harry Elmer Barnes, TBR's mission is to separate historical truth from propaganda and to bring history into accord with the facts.

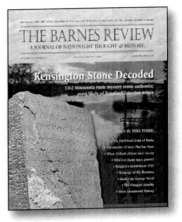

Founded in 1994 by veteran American nationalist Willis A. Carto—a personal friend of Barnes—*The Barnes Review* concurs with Rousseau's maxim that "Falsification of history has done more to impede human development than any one thing known to mankind." TBR covers all aspects of history from the dawn of man to recent events and also places a special focus on the philosophy of nationalism.

As such, TBR proudly describes itself as a "journal of nationalist thought" and dares to be politically incorrect in a day when Cultural Marxism prevails in the mass media, in academia and in day-to-day life. TBR's editorial board of advisors encompasses historians, philosophers and academics from all over the face of the planet, intellectuals united in their desire to bring peace to the world by exposing the lies and prevarications of the past that have brought us to where we are today.

If you believe everything you see in the "responsible" media or think that absolutely everything that appears in most college-level history texts is true, you might be shocked by what you see in TBR—but if you are shocked by what you see in TBR, then that's all the more reason you need to join the growing ranks of independent-minded free-thinkers from all walks of life and all over the world who are longtime TBR subscribers.

Isn't it time you subscribe?

THE BARNES REVIEW $46 for ONE year (six bimonthly issues—64 pages each);

Call 1-877-773-9077 today and charge a subscription to Visa or MasterCard.

Send your check, money order or credit card information (including expiration date) to:

The BARNES REVIEW
P.O. Box 15877
Washington, D.C. 20003
TOLL FREE: 1-877-773-9077

International Rates: Canada/Mexico—$65 per year. All other nations—$80 per year via air mail.

Check us out at www.barnesreview.org.

Lots of rare, hard-to-find, uncensored books and videos are available!

SUBSCRIBE TO *AMERICAN FREE PRESS* NEWSPAPER AND GET FREE GIFTS!

AMERICAN FREE PRESS ORDERING COUPON

Item#	Description/Title	Qty	Cost Ea.	Total
			SUBTOTAL	
	S&H: No S&H inside U.S. Outside U.S. add $6 per book			
	Send a 1-year subscription to AFP for $59 plus 1 free book*			
	Send a 2-year subscription to AFP for $99 plus 2 free books**			
			TOTAL	

*NOTE ABOUT FREE GIFTS: For a one-year subscription to *American Free Press* newspaper ($59), we'll send you one free copy of AFP's *CITIZENS HANDBOOK*. **For a two-year subscription we'll send you AFP's *CITIZENS HANDBOOK* PLUS *9/11: WHAT REALLY HAPPENED*—$16 in free publications (domestic USA only).

PAYMENT (circle choice):   CHECK/MO   VISA   MC   AMEX   DISCOVER

Card # _____

Expiration Date _____ Signature _____

CUSTOMER INFORMATION: FM510

NAME _____

ADDRESS _____

CIty/STATE/ZIP _____

RETURN WITH PAYMENT TO: AMERICAN FREE PRESS, 645 Pennsylvania Avenue SE, Suite 100, Washington, D.C. 20003. Call 1-888-699-NEWS (6397) toll free to charge a subscription or books to Visa or MasterCard.

FRONTMAN

OBAMA'S DARKEST SECRETS REVEALED

I n 2008, Barack Obama became the face of hope and change. Yet lurking behind the scenes is a host of personages who long ago selected this man to forward their global agenda. *Frontman* reveals the actual powers behind his throne: Bilderberg plotters, Zionist handlers, global financiers and Marxist activists.

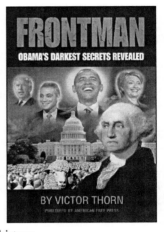

Critics have called Obama an empty suit, but in actuality, the suit is filled by a cabal of men and women whose primary goal is to radically transform the United States. To cover their tracks, an air of secrecy has enveloped Obama's past, including his birth records, college transcripts and employment history.

While other books merely scratch the surface, *Frontman* tears away the deceptive smoke and mirrors that have been used to propel him into the Oval Office. By far the most comprehensive expose to date, President Barack Obama can no longer hide behind a façade that had been carefully created and orchestrated over the past few decades by people who are still pulling his strings. The title says it all: America's commander-in-chief is merely a figurehead for much more powerful people and forces.

Now, at long last, one of the most brutally honest portraits ever presented shows how our nation is being controlled by unseen hands that are leading us perilously close to disaster.

FRONTMAN: Softcover, 112 pages, #O, $20. Available from AMERICAN FREE PRESS, 645 Pennsylvania Avenue SE, #100, Washington, D.C. 20003. No charge for S&H inside the U.S. Call 1-888-699-6397 toll free to charge.

LaVergne, TN USA
11 November 2010
204489LV00001B/6/P